40 Days of Spiritual Awareness

*Becoming aware of how God is
working in and around you.*

Sheila Alewine
Around The Corner Ministries

www.aroundthecornerministries.org

Around The Corner Ministries exists to take the gospel to every neighborhood in America. Our mission is to equip followers of Jesus to engage their neighborhoods and communities with the gospel of Jesus Christ.

ISBN: 978-0-9991318-0-0

Scripture quotations taken from the New American Standard Bible® (NASB), Copyright © 1960, 1962, 1963, 1968, 1971, 1972, 1973, 1975, 1977, 1995 by The Lockman Foundation. Used by permission. www.Lockman.org.

Introduction

What does it mean to be "spiritually aware?" To be aware is to be mindful, or conscious of something. The opposite is to be "oblivious." How often do we walk through our daily life oblivious to the work that God is doing around us? We desire His presence in our lives, and want to be part of His kingdom purposes, but our minds are so focused on the distractions of our world, we miss Him.

This devotional journey is designed to increase your spiritual awareness of who God is and how He is working in the people right around you, and to encourage you to join Him in this work. Each day, you will discover truth that will increase your awareness of God, yourself, other believers, and unbelievers.

Here are some of the things we'll focus on, to improve our **SPIRITUAL AWARENESS**.

Attributes of God: Becoming more aware of who God is, and how He works.
Walking in Him: Increasing our intimacy and awareness of God through prayer.
Attentive to the Holy Spirit: Learning to be aware of His promptings.
Ready to engage others: Serving others in obedience and awareness of the Holy Spirit.
Evangelize: Awareness of opportunities to share the gospel story.

I don't know about you, but the longer I walk with the Lord, the more I realize my need to be reminded about what is important. Unless I consciously focus my heart and mind through daily interaction with His Word, I am easily distracted. That's what this devotional will do for you – remind you of what is important: an awareness of God's work in our world, as He redeems and saves, and how you are an important part of accomplishing that work.

2 Peter 1:12 – *Therefore, I will always be ready to remind you of these things, even though you already know them, and have been established in the truth which is present with you.*

God bless you as you begin this 40-day journey. I pray for God to speak to you through His word, and that you will be renewed and encouraged as you become an ambassador for the gospel.

Sheila Alewine

An Awareness of the Harvest
Day 1 – Day 5

Jesus said to them, "My food is to do the will of Him who sent Me
and to accomplish His work.
Do you not say, 'There are yet four months, and then comes the harvest?'
Behold, I say to you, lift up your eyes and look on the fields,
that they are white for harvest."
John 4:34-35

One of the first steps to a growing awareness of the spiritual work of
God is to recognize the harvest. Jesus' analogy to a physical harvest
is given in the context of sharing the good news of salvation
with the Samaritan woman at the well.

God was working right in front of the disciples, calling men and women
into relationship with Him.
They simply had to **lift up their eyes** and see it.
In the same way, He is calling us to look around us –
where we live, work and play – and see the harvest.

Take It In

*For the Son of Man has come to seek and to save that which was **lost**.*
Luke 19:10

Think It Through

Jesus came for the *lost*.

What does it mean to be lost? In our culture, we understand "lost" to mean "misplaced." We lose our keys; we lose our reading glasses. It can be a temporary loss, such as when we realize we put our keys into the freezer when we put away the ice cream after a trip to the grocery store.

But the Bible's use of the word "lost" has a greater meaning. The word is *apollymi*. It means "to destroy, to kill, or to perish." It is the same word used in John 3:16, but is translated *perish*. It is not simply a temporary situation, but a condition, a state of being. Without Christ's intervention, without His willingness to enter our world, the human race is perishing. It is lost.

Jesus used several parables to illustrate the concept of *lostness*; a lost sheep (Luke 15:1-7), a lost coin (Luke 15:8-10), the prodigal son (Luke 15:11-32). In each of these, there is a common theme of great joy when the lost one is found. The joy is great, because the condition of *lostness* is severe. It is an obstacle that can only be overcome by someone acting on the one who is lost. A lost sheep will not find its way home: it is bewildered. A lost coin has no life in itself to return to its owner: it is dead. A lost son will not see the answer to his condition until his eyes are opened: he is blind.

Live It Out

Do you realize that before Christ came, you were perishing? You had no hope of spiritual life. Your condition was irreversible by your own strength. You were lost, just as millions of people today who have not experienced the hope of salvation. Jesus came for you, because you were lost.

As you go about your day today, look around you. Let God's Spirit remind you of your previous condition. What would your life be if Jesus had not come for the lost?

John 3:16 – *For God so loved the world, that He gave His only begotten Son, that whoever believes in Him shall not **perish**, but have eternal life.*

PRAY TODAY:
Dear Jesus, I thank You that You saw my lostness. And I am so grateful that You came into this world for those who were lost … for me. I realize that I could do nothing to change my lostness. Without You, I would die and be separated from You forever. You acted. Thank You for coming to seek and to save the ones who are perishing. Let my heart be Your heart for those who are still lost. Amen.

Day Two: Jesus came to seek the lost.

Take It In

*For the Son of Man has come to **seek** and to save that which was lost.*
Luke 19:10

Think It Through

Many years ago, I was shopping with a friend, and her precocious red-headed two-year-old son, when we experienced a mother's worst nightmare. We were browsing among the racks of clothing when she suddenly realized that her son was not in her sight. I heard her, from across the store, begin to call his name. By the time she had to repeat his name the fifth time, she was close to hysterical and was yelling loudly. I could see the panic in her eyes, and hear it in her voice. *He was lost.*

Thankfully, we found him shortly afterwards; as most kids would, he thought it was fun to play **hide and seek**. There was relief, joy, frustration, and tears.

The word "seek" means "to seek after, seek for, aim at, strive after." Do you realize that Jesus sought you? That He still seeks the lost? I don't believe Jesus is in panic mode, like my friend, because God always knows exactly where we are. Instead, Jesus seeks us intentionally, as He pursues us relentlessly. He comes after us. He knows that unless He comes for us, we will remain in our lostness, deceived into thinking we are hiding from God.

Jesus is striving after the lost. Just as Jesus physically walked this earth, speaking, teaching, inviting people to believe, to listen, and to respond, His Spirit is at work in those who are lost. He is calling out to those who are tired of hiding, and are ready to come home.

Live It Out

Who have you met lately that needs to come home? How can you be part of their journey back towards God? Put yourself back in the position of the one who was lost. What would you want someone to do for you?

2 Peter 3:9 - *The Lord is not slow about His promise, as some count slowness, but is patient toward you, not wishing for any to **perish** but for all to come to repentance.*

PRAY TODAY:
Dear Jesus, Thank You for seeking me. Thank You that You did not leave me in my lostness, but pursued me in patience, in love, and in mercy. You came after me. You called out my name, so that I would respond to You. You acted on my heart, giving me faith to believe. If you had not sought me, I would still be lost. Oh, Father, give me Your heart for those who are still lost. I want to be used as Your vessel, as You pursue those who are perishing. Amen.

Day Three: Jesus came to save the lost.

Take It In

*And Jesus said to him, "Today **salvation** has come to this house, because he, too, is a son of Abraham. For the Son of Man has come to seek and to **save** that which was lost."* Luke 19:9-10

Think It Through

Jesus came to pursue us, to seek us out, for a specific purpose – salvation. He had a **mission** to accomplish, the saving of our souls. We might say Luke 19:10 was the "mission statement" of His earthly life, and that mission culminated at the Cross.

Why do men need saving? What are we saved from?

The word "save" in scripture means "to preserve one who is in danger of destruction, to save or rescue." Men are born separated from God, destined for destruction. We are born to perish. Sin has caused a great divide between us and our Creator, and without salvation, it is impossible to reach heaven, and be restored to a right relationship with God.

Romans 5:8-9 tells us exactly what we are saved from: *the wrath of God.* Jesus came to place Himself in the path of God's wrath against sin; He was judged guilty in our place and took on Himself our punishment. The cross was the destination of Jesus' mission, given to Him by His Father, and He completed it.

Jesus' mission on yesterday's cross becomes our mission in today's culture.

Live It Out

Jesus' earthly mission ended at the cross, but ours begins with it. The gift of salvation is an end to an old way of life, and a beginning of a life with new purpose: to bring others to the cross so that they, too, can be saved from the wrath of God. Look around you. What neighbor, co-worker or friend do you know who is destined for destruction? Ask God to show you how to tell them the good news that Jesus came to save.

Romans 5:8-9 – *But God demonstrates His own love toward us, in that while we were yet sinners, Christ died for us. Much more then, having now been justified by His blood, we shall be saved from the wrath of God through Him.*

John 3:17 – *For God did not send the Son into the world to judge the world, but that the world might be saved through Him.*

PRAY TODAY:
Dear Jesus, Thank You for completing Your mission, and accomplishing salvation for the world. You rescued me...from my sin, from my own selfish desires, and from eternal destruction. Unless You had sought me out, and brought salvation, I would be eternally lost and separated from You. Help me to see that others who have not responded to Your offer of salvation are perishing. Use me to tell the world that You have come to save us. Amen.

Day Four: Jesus sends out the laborers.

Take It In

*Now after this the Lord **appointed** seventy others, and sent them in pairs ahead of Him to every city and place where He Himself was going to come. And He was saying to them, "The harvest is plentiful, but the laborers are few; therefore beseech the Lord of the harvest to **send out** laborers into His harvest."*
Luke 10:1-2

Think It Through

Jesus is coming.

Did you catch that phrase?

Jesus sent His disciples ahead of Him to all the places *where He Himself was going to come.* This was no trivial assignment. It was a mission. Jesus had plans to visit these villages and cities, and He sent His followers – those who already believed in Him – ahead of Him. Why were they being sent?

The harvest was ready. God was already at work in the hearts of the people they would meet. They were given the privilege of introducing them to Jesus. Wherever Jesus sends us, He is coming right behind our words, our actions, and our prayers, to meet the spiritual hunger of the lost.

What if you were in charge of preparing a city for a visit from the President of the United States? Think of the details that would need to be covered: security, schedule, lodging, restaurant reservations, invitations to the proper people. In contrast, all Jesus asks is that we go ahead of Him, speaking the truth of the gospel, acting in ways that reflect His love and holiness, showing mercy and grace. Then He comes. He comes to the harvest that He has prepared.

Live It Out

Where has Jesus sent you? He is coming! Are you willing to be Christ's ambassador, preparing the way for Him?

2 Corinthians 5:20 - *Therefore, we are ambassadors for Christ, as though God were making an appeal through us; we beg you on behalf of Christ, be reconciled to God.*

PRAY TODAY:
Dear Jesus, I am thankful You came to me. And I am excited that You are coming to the people who live around me – in my neighborhood, at my office, and everywhere I go. Help me to prepare the way, just as Your disciples did when You were here. I believe that Your Spirit is at work in others. Thank You for the privilege of telling others that You have come for them. Amen.

Day Five: Sowing and reaping the harvest.

Take It In

For in this case the saying is true, 'One sows and another reaps.' I sent you to reap that for which you have not labored; others have labored and you have entered into their labor.
John 4:37-38

Think It Through

My husband, a pastor, tells the story of a man who called him and asked for an appointment. He wanted to talk about becoming a Christian, about accepting God's free gift of salvation. Of course, the appointment was made as soon as possible. When the man came in the next day, they began talking about what it meant to become a Christian. There was no delay in the man's response. He was so ready to accept Christ, my husband said it was like fruit falling off a tree. God had already done the work in the man's heart. Like a baby ready to be born, he was just there to witness it.

This is what Jesus means when He speaks of entering into another's labor. The work of the harvest is done over a period of months. First, the ground must be tilled and prepared. Then the seed must be planted. This is followed by weeks of watering, sunshine, and fertilizing at the proper time. Then, when the wheat has matured and is ready, the harvesters come.

As we love others, pray for them, share our story, serve them through good deeds, and tell the good news of the gospel, we are all sharing in the same harvest. Sometimes God calls us to plant the first seed – the first time a person hears the gospel. Others may water and fertilize the seed, through prayer, good works, loving and showing grace. Then, when the Lord of the harvest determines the proper time, they will be born into the kingdom.

Live It Out

What part of the harvest are you working in today? Be conscious of sharing wherever you are – you may be getting ready to reap where another has already sown!

Galatians 6:9 - *Let us not lose heart in doing good, for in due time we will **reap** if we do not grow weary.*

PRAY TODAY:
Dear Jesus, I am a product of many people sowing the seeds of the gospel into my heart. Some people prayed. Some people told me the stories of the Bible. Some people were kind and gracious and loving toward me when I did not deserve it. Others showed me what real forgiveness looked like. All of these things grew in me and bore the fruit of salvation. Thank You for all the people You put in my life that had a part in my journey to salvation. Let me be conscious of being that person for others who have not yet come into Your kingdom. Amen.

An Awareness of the Sovereignty of God
Day 6 – Day 9

The Lord has established His throne in the heavens,
and His sovereignty rules over all. Bless the Lord, you His angels, mighty in
strength, who perform His word, obeying the voice of His word!
Bless the Lord, all you His hosts,
you who serve Him, doing His will.
Bless the Lord, all you works of His, in all places of His dominion;
bless the Lord, O my soul!
Psalm 103:19-22

God's sovereignty rules over all!
All of creation is designed to perform His word, obey His voice,
and serve Him, doing His will. We are the work of His hands.

As we grow in our spiritual awareness, we begin to understand that
God has a purpose for us. He has dominion over all the earth,
and has sovereignly put us where He desires.
For what purpose?
To make Him known, as we labor in the harvest that He has set before
our eyes. We are part of His divine plan.

What a glorious and encouraging truth – we are chosen to serve the
Most High God, Creator and Master of all. Bless the Lord, O my soul!

Day Six: God is sovereign in where we live.

Take It In

And He made from one man every nation of mankind to live on all the face of the earth, having determined their appointed times and the boundaries of their habitation, that they would seek God, if perhaps they might grope for Him and find Him, though He is not far from each one of us; for in Him we live and move and exist. Acts 17:26-28

Think It Through

This scripture teaches that God has sovereignly determined the placement of all nations. The word used for "nation" is *ethnos*, from which we get our word "ethnic." It speaks not only of nations as a country, but even more specifically as "people groups" – those united by language, custom, location, religion, and common history. According to *The Joshua Project* website, there are approximately 16,650 people groups in the world, more than 7 billion individuals!

If God has sovereignly placed men in pre-determined places, it naturally follows that He must have a purpose, a design. We see that purpose in verse 27: *that they would seek God.* God has put a desire for Himself in every human being, although as unbelievers, we do not recognize that it is *Him* we are seeking. All around you, today, are individuals who have a need and a desire for God, but they do not know how to satisfy that need.

Sometimes God calls individuals to go far away from their home to speak the gospel to unreached people groups in a foreign land. But every believer has a call on their life to speak the words of hope and salvation to those who are right in front of us. When we begin to recognize that God has intentionally orchestrated our lives so that we might engage the harvest in our nation, our city, and our neighborhood, we have begun to recognize that He is sovereign.

Live It Out

Perhaps you are like many who feel unworthy and a bit guilty that you are blessed to live in a first-world nation, in relative comfort, with easy access to the gospel? Instead of questioning God's sovereignty, why not consider that God has a purpose for you right where you live, work and play? Accept this gift of a sovereign God, realizing that He has blessed you so that you can be His hands, His feet, and His voice! **If you are willing to go wherever God leads you, you must also be willing to stay where He has put you.** Commit to being used in this place, at this time, to share the good news with those around you – *those who are seeking God, if perhaps they might grope for Him and find Him, though He is not far from each one of us.* (Acts 17:27)

PRAY TODAY:
Dear Jesus, I worship You because You are a sovereign and holy God. I thank You that You have counted me worthy to hear your salvation message, and You gave me faith to believe the truth. You changed me. Help me to live in the knowledge of Your sovereign activity in my life, and to remember that You have a plan and a purpose for me to be a laborer in the harvest You have placed around me. I want to see my neighbors, my co-workers, my friends and everyone I meet as someone who needs to hear the good news about You. Thank you for letting me be part of Your sovereign kingdom work. Amen.

Day Seven: God's sovereignty displayed in salvation.

Take It In

The Lord has established His throne in the heavens, and His sovereignty rules over all. Psalm 103:19

Think It Through

Sovereignty speaks of having supreme authority or reign.   It is a "kingdom" word, one that speaks of a ruler who has absolute power and authority. It is that attribute of God by which we understand He is intimately involved in the circumstances of our lives, and that He has every right to be, because He rules over us.

The word "sovereign" itself is rarely used in scripture to describe God; its meaning, however, is abundantly clear. Consider just three verses that describe God's sovereignty over our life.

Proverbs 16:9 – *The mind of man plans his way, but the Lord directs His steps.*

Psalm 115:3 – *But our God is in the heavens; He does whatever He pleases.*

2 Chronicles 20:6 – *O Lord, the God of our fathers, are You not God in the heavens? And are You not ruler over all the kingdoms of the nations? Power and might are in Your hand so that no one can stand against You.*

To the unbeliever, it may seem unfair or frightening to think of a supreme being having rule over one's life. But to the believer, there is a sweet sense of peace and security, because we know that God's sovereign nature works in harmony with all of His attributes. God is love, so the sovereign power He wields over our life will always be an act of love. God is holy, so His actions and motives are always pure. He is merciful and gracious, so as we submit to His authority, we are met with mercy and grace.

Think of God's sovereignty in the context of reaching our neighbors with the gospel. As God ***directs our steps***, we meet people with spiritual needs. As we share the message of the gospel, God ***does what He wills, what brings Him pleasure***: His Spirit speaks to their heart through our words and actions. And as the spiritual battle ensues for their mind and heart to surrender to the gospel, God's ***power and might*** acts to draw them into a relationship, into His amazing salvation.

Live It Out

We cannot share the gospel without seeing the sovereignty of God everywhere. The miracle of salvation is only accomplished because our God is sovereign, and He rules the hearts of mankind. Our responsibility is not to make someone believe; we are simply to present the gospel and watch God do His sovereign work.

John 6:44 – No one can come to Me unless the Father who sent Me draws him; and I will raise him up on the last day.

PRAY TODAY:
Dear Jesus, I recognize that You are sovereign...over me, over the world I live in, over every person. I submit to Your authority in my life. I surrender my time, my talents, my resources, and all my hopes and dreams to Your sovereign plans. Let me be used in Your kingdom purposes. I desire to walk in harmony with Your Spirit, and to be a holy vessel that You can speak through to others. Thank You that I can rest in the knowledge that nothing happens in life outside of Your sovereign power and plans. Amen.

Day Eight: God's sovereignty displayed in creation.

Take It In

Worthy are You, our Lord and our God, to receive glory and honor and power; for You created all things, and because of Your will they existed, and were created. Revelation 4:11

In the beginning God created the heavens and the earth. Genesis 1:1

Think It Through

Our God is Creator.

If we begin with an understanding that we were created by God and for God, then the gospel and salvation makes sense. The story of salvation that unfolds in the Bible does not begin when the Savior, Jesus, came to earth. It doesn't begin with Christmas. Salvation begins in Genesis 1:1 – God created. Why did God create this earth simply by speaking it into existence, and then create man out of dust to occupy it? We know that God needs nothing. He is complete in Himself, not lacking anything.

Paul tells us why God created, in Colossians 1:16 – *For by Him all things were created, both in the heavens and on earth, visible and invisible, whether thrones or dominions or rulers or authorities—all things have been created through Him and for Him.*

Man was created for God. In the beginning, before sin entered the world, God and man enjoyed intimate fellowship. Sin spoiled what God originally intended, but this did not surprise God. The answer to man's sin was that God put His plan of salvation into action, a plan He made in eternity past.

Did you get that? God created us, knowing that it would require the life of His Son to accomplish His eternal purpose and plan of fellowship and intimacy and glory between human men and holy God. Because He created us for Himself.

Live It Out

The next time you think that someone you know is beyond the reach of the gospel, remember that God created that person for Himself. He desires them. He longs to show compassion to His creation. God treasured us, His creation, so much so that He willingly gave His Son for our redemption and salvation.

The God who created us is at work in the hearts of people everywhere, *re-creating* individuals who respond to His call. The story of salvation begins with creation, and ends with a new creation.

2 Corinthians 5:17 – *Therefore if anyone is in Christ, he is a new creature; the old things passed away; behold, new things have come. Now all these things are from God, who reconciled us to Himself through Christ and gave us the ministry of reconciliation.*

PRAY TODAY:
Dear Jesus, Thank You for reconciling us to the Father. I am so grateful that You had a plan from eternity past for my salvation. You did not abandon Your creation, but paid the highest price for us to be re-created in Your image, and welcomed back to the relationship with God for which we were created. As You continue to work out Your plan and purpose in my life, let me be a witness for the One who created me. Thank You for creating me. Amen.

Day Nine: God's sovereignty and our free will.

Take It In

For this is the will of My Father that everyone who beholds the Son and believes in Him will have eternal life, and I Myself will raise him up on the last day. John 6:40

The Lord is not slow about His promise, as some count slowness, but is patient toward you, not wishing for any to perish but for all to come to repentance. 2 Peter 3:9

Think It Through

How does the sovereignty of God reconcile with the free will of man, both concepts taught in scripture?

This is a question that great theologians have debated for centuries, in an attempt to understand these seemingly contradictory statements.

Scripture clearly teaches that God chooses the elect, those that come to know Him (Ephesian 1). But it also teaches that man must respond by repentance and belief (John 5-6).

Salvation itself is a mystery, for who can truly explain how the Spirit of God can change a man's heart? Why should we diminish the glory of God's gospel by dissecting it according to our human logic?

Picture salvation as a door. Before we experience salvation, we are on the outside, standing before the door. God draws us. He convicts us. He speaks to our heart, wooing and convincing us of the truth of the gospel. He opens our eyes. From our perspective, we must act. We must respond by repenting of our sin and believing in the work of Christ on the cross. On this side of salvation, it seems we must reach for the doorknob, open the door, and step through.

On the other side of the door, we look back. We now stand in salvation. We have experienced the work of God's Spirit on our heart, and mind, and soul. We realize that we never possessed the power to open the door: *it was all God.* We were dead in our sins, with no ability to raise ourselves to spiritual life. At all times, it was God moving on us, regenerating us, bringing our spirit to life so that we could respond to Him. Our perspective has changed, and we now understand the sovereignty of God that brought us to salvation.

Live It Out

If salvation is accomplished only by the sovereignty of God, is it necessary that we share the gospel? Can God not accomplish it without us? I believe that would be exactly what our enemy, Satan, would want us to think.

This one thing we know: The last instruction Christ gave His followers was to go and make disciples of all nations (Matthew 28:19-20). According to John 6:40, men must behold the Son to believe in Him, so this is our task, to present the Son. We will leave the questions of *how* salvation happens to God, and go in faith and obedience to tell a dying world that Jesus saves.

Romans 10:9-10 – *That if you confess with your mouth Jesus as Lord, and believe in your heart that God raised Him from the dead; you will be saved; for with the heart a person believes, resulting in righteousness, and with the mouth he confesses, resulting in salvation.*

PRAY TODAY:

Dear Jesus, I thank You and adore You because You are a sovereign God. I had no power to save myself, and it is only because Your Holy Spirit convicted me of my sin, opened my eyes, and regenerated my spirit, that I stand in Your salvation. Thank You for drawing me, and for wanting me. Let my life be an act of obedience as I tell others of the wonderful things that You have done. Use my words and actions to draw others to Yourself. Amen.

An Awareness of the Power of Prayer
Day 10 – Day 14

For this reason also, since the day we heard of it,
we have not ceased to pray for you and to ask that you may be filled with
the knowledge of His will in all spiritual wisdom and understanding,
so that you will walk in a manner worthy of the Lord,
to please Him in all respects, bearing fruit in every good work
and increasing in the knowledge of God.
Colossians 1:9-10

The author of these words, Paul the apostle, knew about the power of
prayer. He loved his fellow believers at Colossae, and desired for them
to grow strong in their faith and be able to stand firm in the face of
persecution. His choice would have been to be with them, face to face,
but God had a different plan for Paul at this time.
He was in prison.

Paul's circumstances did not hinder him, however.
He knew the *secret of influence.*
It was not his presence or his teaching ability. It was the power of
prayer.

As we grow in awareness of how God does the miraculous work of
changing hearts, we discover the power of praying boldly, persistently,
and specifically.

Day Ten: Asking God for a heart to pray.

Take It In

I am telling the truth in Christ, I am not lying, my conscience testifies with me in the Holy Spirit, that I have great sorrow and unceasing grief in my heart. For I could wish that I myself were accursed, separated from Christ for the sake of my brethren, my kinsmen according to the flesh. ... Brethren, my heart's desire and my prayer to God for them is for their salvation.
Romans 9:1-3; Romans 10:3

Think It Through

Paul's heart was broken for his fellow Jews who rejected Christ. While he held them fully accountable for rejecting the truth that they had been given, his heart ached for them to come to know Christ, so much that he was willing to be condemned himself if it would convince them of the truth.

The words Paul uses for "great sorrow" and "unceasing grief" speak of pain, of body or mind; it is a state of mourning – a consuming grief. He felt physical pain when he thought about the separation between God and his fellow religious Jews. Even though these were the very people who caused him suffering and affliction, rejecting his message of salvation through Jesus, he longed for them to come to a saving knowledge of the truth.

What did Paul do with this grief and sorrow? He turned it into prayer. He says that his heart's desire is for their salvation. The word "desire" means good pleasure, satisfaction or delight. His greatest delight, what would bring him great pleasure, would be for his enemies to come to Christ. He took the desire of his heart and presented it to God in prayer.

Live It Out

Does your heart ache when you think of people around you who do not know Christ? Or do you think lightly of the eternal consequences of a living a life in rebellion against God, and dying without knowing the Savior? The eternal destiny of those who reject Jesus is understandably something that we do not like to think or talk about, but it should cause our hearts to be broken for those who are lost. Ask God to give you, like

Paul, His heart's desire to see unbelievers come to salvation, and a heart that is committed to pray for them.

1 Corinthians 6:9-10 – *Or do you not know that the unrighteous will not inherit the kingdom of God? Do not be deceived; neither fornicators, nor idolaters nor adulterers, nor homosexuals, nor thieves, nor the covetous, nor drunkards, nor revilers, nor swindlers, will inherit the kingdom of God.*

PRAY TODAY:
Dear Jesus, I confess that I have thought too little of the eternal destiny of those who do not know you. I ask You to give me a tender heart that grieves over the lost. Give me a burden to pray for them. Forgive me when I get too wrapped up in my own blessed life with You, that I fail to pray for those who have not yet come to believe! Amen.

Day Eleven: Praying for God to open eyes.

Take It In

I pray that the eyes of your heart may be enlightened, so that you will know what is the hope of His calling, what are the riches of the glory of His inheritance in the saints, and what is the surpassing greatness of His power toward us who believe. Ephesians 1:18-19a

For God, who said, "Light shall shine out of darkness," is the One who has shone in our hearts to give the Light of the knowledge of the glory of God in the face of Christ. 2 Corinthians 4:6

Think It Through

What do we pray for the unbeliever? What specific things should we ask God for as we bring our neighbors, co-workers and friends before His throne?

We pray for the light to come on!

Have you ever gotten up at night without turning on the lights? If the room is dark, you tread lightly, with hands out in front of you, feeling your way along and hoping that you do not run into any obstacles. This is exactly what it is like to try to explain salvation to someone whose spiritual eyes have not been opened. They might listen to what you are saying, but will try to "feel" their way into understanding truth.

One way to pray for others is to ask God to open their spiritual eyes. Unless God shines the light in their heart, and opens their understanding, they will not be able to receive truth. We must ask God to cause them to see truth, and He will answer by sending His Spirit to open their eyes.

Live It Out

Pray diligently and specifically for those to whom you are witnessing, that God will give them the light of the knowledge of Christ. Pray that they will see and believe.

1 Corinthians 2:14 – *But a natural man does not accept the things of the Spirit of God, for they are foolishness to him; and he cannot understand them, because they are spiritually appraised.*

PRAY TODAY:
Dear Jesus, There are so many around me today who observe the evidence of Your work and Your redemption, but still do not see and understand. I can testify to them about You, but unless You open their eyes, they will not believe. I pray today that You will open their eyes, and give them spiritual sight to see their sinful condition. I ask that You grant them understanding, and that You shine the light of the glory of Yourself so that they will believe. Amen.

Day Twelve: Praying for boldness.

Take It In

And pray on my behalf, that utterance may be given to me in the opening of my mouth, to make known with boldness the mystery of the gospel, for which I am an ambassador in chains; that in proclaiming it I may speak boldly, as I ought to speak.
Ephesians 6:19-20

Think It Through

Does it surprise you that Paul felt it necessary to ask for the believers to pray for him to be bold?

Our picture of Paul is one of fearlessness and confidence. He spoke before kings and the highest ruling priests in the Jewish temple. His pedigree was impeccable, a Hebrew of Hebrews, blameless in keeping the law. Outwardly, he had every reason to be confident and bold. Yet, it was something he felt he needed God's help to be.

The word used for "boldness" in this scripture has the dual meanings of "openly and freely" as well as "fearless confidence." Paul was not only asking for the confidence to speak the gospel, but that he would be transparent and natural in his conversations with others. To speak openly and freely is to speak sincerely, without pretense. Paul wanted the people to which he spoke to know that he was sincere, as well as to have the courage and confidence to talk to anyone, anytime anywhere, about Jesus.

If Paul felt it necessary to pray for boldness, how much more should we ask God to give us boldness?

Live It Out

How do we grow in our boldness as witnesses of the gospel? Where do we get our confidence? A great example is that of Peter and John, after they were filled with the Spirit at Pentecost. The Spirit of God empowers us to speak. He gives us the words and directs our thoughts. As we grow in our own faith, our conversations about God will be a natural, unpretentious overflow of what is in our heart, and as we obey the Spirit's promptings to speak to others, we will gain confidence and boldness.

Acts 4:13 – *Now as they observed the confidence of Peter and John and understood that they were uneducated and untrained men, they were amazed, and began to recognize them as having been with Jesus.*

PRAY TODAY:
Dear Jesus, I ask for boldness. Just like Peter, John, and Paul, I want to be a mighty witness to others. I want to speak boldly about your salvation, and I want others to know that I am sincere. I ask that Your Spirit would empower me. Speak to my heart the words that You would have me speak to others. Give me confidence and boldness in knowing that the gospel is the power of salvation, and must be proclaimed so that unbelievers may come to know the truth. Amen.

Day Thirteen: Persistent prayers.

Take It In

Devote yourselves to prayer, keeping alert in it with an attitude of thanksgiving; praying at the same time for us as well, that God will open up to us a door for the word, so that we may speak forth the mystery of Christ, for which I have also been imprisoned; that I may make it clear in the way I ought to speak.
Colossians 4:2-4

Think It Through

After we have prayed for God to open the spiritual eyes of our neighbors and co-workers, and have asked Him for boldness to speak freely and openly, now we must ask God for an opportunity.

Have you ever spent time with someone who you know needs to hear the gospel, but can't seem to get the conversation around to spiritual things? Do you ever feel defeated, like you wasted the moment? That you used your time to talk about things that have no eternal value? Paul must have experienced this, because he asked the believers to pray for open doors. An open door is simply an indication that the person you are speaking with is interested in spiritual things, and possibly open to hearing the gospel.

Every person we meet has a history with God. It may be "ancient" history. They may have good memories of visiting a church as a child, or they may have experienced hurt and rejection from those who claimed to know and love God. Or, they may never have heard of God, even though He has been right there watching over them and drawing them to Himself their entire life. We can't see into a person's heart, but God can. This is why we pray for God to open the door of a person's heart to hear the word. As He gives us opportunities, we plant the seeds of hope and salvation, trusting that in God's time, they will bear fruit.

Live It Out

Praying for God to open the heart of someone to hear words of truth is an act of love. It takes time, patience and persistence. Paul tells the Colossian believers, *devote yourselves to prayer*. We should never underestimate the power of prayer in reaching others for Christ. God must do His work in the heart so that the seeds we sow will take root.

1 Thessalonians 5:17 – *Pray without ceasing.*

PRAY TODAY:
Dear Jesus, Thank You for opening the door of my heart to hear the gospel. Someone once told me about You, and because You were already working in my heart, I was ready to hear it. Thank You for those faithful believers who prayed for me before I knew You. Help me to be a prayer warrior for others. Let me remember that before I speak to others about You, I need to speak to You about them. Help me be faithful to depend on You to do Your amazing work in their heart, and then seize the opportunity to share the good news. Amen.

Day Fourteen: Battle prayers (this is war).

Take It In

And even if our gospel is veiled, it is veiled to those who are perishing, in whose case the god of this world has blinded the minds of the unbelieving so that they might not see the light of the gospel of the glory of Christ, who is the image of God.
2 Corinthians 4:3-4

With gentleness correcting those who are in opposition, if perhaps God may grant them repentance leading to the knowledge of the truth, and that they may come to their senses and escape from the snare of the devil, having been held captive by him to do his will.
2 Timothy 2:25-26

Think It Through

Whenever we commit to begin sharing the gospel with our friends and neighbors, we must be prepared for the spiritual warfare that will follow. Our enemy, Satan, hates the gospel, for it is the gospel which frees man from his control. As long as a man remains outside the kingdom of God, Satan can deceive him, blinding him to the truth, and keeping him content in his own self-image and self-worship. But once the light of the gospel begins to expose the enemy's lies, war is declared.

Consider the phrase "come to their senses and escape from the snare of the devil." It is said that a common practice during this time was to scatter seeds laced with an additive that caused drowsiness in order to make birds easier to snare. They would find themselves in a stupor, almost as if drunk, and so the fowler could easily throw the net over them to ensnare them. This is the picture of how Satan blinds the mind of the unbeliever to the truth, and entangles them in worldly pursuits, so that they do not even realize the spiritual danger.

We must pray specifically for God to awaken men and women who are trapped in spiritual darkness. We must pray for God to protect them from Satan's schemes, and for God to act to rescue them from Satan's kingdom. Our God is more powerful than the enemy!

Live It Out

Who do you know that is trapped by the schemes and snares of the enemy? It may be a physical addiction, such as alcohol or drugs, that deadens the mind and keeps the heart from feeling the conviction of the Spirit of God. It may be a lie that has them convinced they are doing well, unaware of the spiritual dangers ahead. Pray boldly for God to stand against Satan's plans. Pray for God to awaken them from their spiritual sleep before it is too late.

Ephesians 5:13-14 - *But all things become visible when they are exposed by the light, for everything that becomes visible is light. For this reason it says, "Awake, sleeper, and arise from the dead, and Christ will shine on you."*

PRAY TODAY:
Dear Jesus, I thank You that You are more powerful than our enemy. Nothing and no one can stand against You. I pray boldly for those who are caught in the snare of deception. I ask you to show Yourself mighty on their behalf, to break through the hardness of their heart, and reveal Yourself to them. Thank You that You rescued me from my own deceptions. Use me to show others how powerful and loving You are by the way I live and speak. Amen.

An Awareness of the Holy Spirit
Day 15 – Day 20

I will ask the Father, and He will give you another Helper,
that He may be with you forever; that is the Spirit of truth,
whom the world cannot receive, because it does not see Him or know Him,
but you know Him because He abides with you and will be in you.
John 14:16-17

If you knew you were going to leave someone you loved very much,
what would be the last thing you would tell them? Jesus' words in John
14 were given to His disciples on the night before He went to the cross.
They are words of comfort and encouragement.
Jesus wanted them to know that they would not be alone.

The promise of the indwelling Spirit of God was the very best news,
because He intended the disciples to continue His work after He left
them to return to heaven. He knew they could not do this work without
the power of God directing them, guiding them and enabling them.
This is the Spirit's work.

As we grow in awareness of our mission to reach the lost,
we must learn to listen closely to and depend on the Holy Spirit.

Day Fifteen: The power of the Spirit to be a witness.

Take It In

But you will receive power when the Holy Spirit has come upon you; and you shall be My witnesses both in Jerusalem, and in all Judea and Samaria, and even to the remotest part of the earth.
Acts 1:8

Think It Through

The word Jesus uses for "power" is the Greek word *dynamis*, from which we get our English "dynamite." It has the meaning of inherent power, power which resides within, power residing in a thing by virtue of its nature.

Do you see what Jesus is saying? The power to witness comes from the power which resides within us, but not from ourselves. The disciples did not possess the power to be His witnesses, because the Holy Spirit had not yet come to reside in them. The power of God would take up residence in human men, and as a result, they would go out into the world and be Christ's witnesses.

Have you ever turned on a lamp, but nothing happens? No light appears? You immediately know that one of two things is wrong: either the bulb is burned out, or the lamp is unplugged. Because the rest of your house is functioning normally (the power has not gone out), you know that the source of power is perfectly adequate to turn on the lamp. So the answer is either the bulb or the connection.

In some ways, this is an accurate illustration. When the power source meets the filament in the bulb, it shines. It has no choice but to give off the light for which it was created. When you accepted God's gift of salvation, the Holy Spirit, your source of power, came to live within you, and your life becomes a light – a witness, of the power of God. God's Spirit *never* leaves us; the power is always there. If we fail to shine, then we must examine our connection to God. Sin, fear, apathy, or simple disobedience can cause our light to dim.

Live It Out

How do we "reconnect" to God and allow God's Spirit to empower us to be mighty witnesses of His salvation? We get rid of anything that has broken our fellowship with God by repentance and confession, and we make sure we are "plugged in" – time in His Word, time in talking to Him and listening to Him in prayer. Jesus gave us the gift of His Holy Spirit to empower our lives. We must surrender our lives and let His power do the work.

Luke 24:48-49 – *You are witnesses of these things. And behold, I am sending forth the promise of My Father upon you; but you are to stay in the city until you are clothed with power from on high.*

PRAY TODAY:
Dear Jesus, I confess that I have often tried to be Your witness in my own power. I have failed to remember that Your Spirit indwells me – a gift You gave me when You saved me, and that only when I am surrendered to His power can I be used to shine Your light in this world. Keep me from sin or any distraction that would dim the light of Your glory in my life. Teach me to listen to Your Spirit, and allow Him to shine through me to a world that needs Your salvation. Amen.

Day Sixteen: The prompts of the Spirit to act.

Take It In

Then the Spirit said to Philip, "Go up and join this chariot." Philip ran up and heard him reading Isaiah the prophet, and said, "Do you understand what you are reading?" And he said, "Well, how could I unless someone guides me?" And he invited Philip to come up and sit with him.
Acts 8:29-31a

Think It Through

Have you ever heard someone use the word "serendipity?" It was coined in the 1700's from a Persian fairytale called *The Three Princes of Serendip*, whose heroes were "always making discoveries by accident, of things they were not in quest of." The word has come to mean good fortune or luck.

Do you think it was "luck" or "serendipity" that Philip just happened to be at the right place, at the right time, to meet the Ethiopian eunuch in Acts 8, or that the man just happened to be reading the prophet Isaiah, wishing he had someone to explain it to him? We know it was a moment orchestrated by a sovereign God, whose had directed Philip to be on that Gaza road, for the particular purpose of sharing the gospel with this man.

Does God still do this today? I believe He does!

Some time ago I was walking in my neighborhood, thinking and praying about two specific neighbors. I wanted the opportunity to get to know them better, with the ultimate hope of sharing Christ with them through my actions and words. As I crested the hill, lo and behold, those two neighbors were just beginning a walk and invited me to join them. Was this accidental? Serendipity? I believe it was an answer to my prayer. God's Spirit had prompted me to be thinking about them and praying for them. Then He put us all three together for a walk.

My quest that day was not to meet someone. It was simply to take a walk, and spend time listening to God and praying for those He brought to mind. My quest was following after Jesus, to know Him. As we pursue our relationship with God, He will put us exactly where we need to be, to accomplish what He desires.

Live It Out

If God brings someone to your mind to pray for, it's not accidental or coincidence. He is at work, and our role is simply to join Him in it. And don't be surprised when that person you've been praying for is right before you when you least expect it.

Listen when God's Spirit prompts. Trust Him to put you in places and circumstances that are God-designed, divine moments.

Acts 13:52 – *And the disciples were continually filled with joy and with the Holy Spirit.*

PRAY TODAY:
Dear Jesus, Thank You for the gift of Your Holy Spirit, who came to indwell me when You saved me. I want to hear You when Your Spirit speaks to me. Sometimes the world is noisy, and crowds out Your still small voice. Teach me a be still, to listen, to hear, and then to act when You speak. I believe

You are at work in the people around me. Use me for Your divine purposes, to be Your spokesperson to those who need to hear Your words. Amen.

Day Seventeen: The words of the Spirit to speak.

Take It In

Behold, I send you out as sheep in the midst of wolves; so be shrewd as serpents and innocent as doves. But beware of men, for they will hand you over to the courts and scourge you in their synagogues; and you will even be brought before governors and kings for My sake as a testimony to them and to the Gentiles. But when they hand you over, do not worry about how or what you are to say; for it will be given you in that hour what you are to say. For it is not you who speak, but it is the Spirit of your Father who speaks in you. Matthew 10:16-20

Think It Through

Are you ever at a loss for words?

Jesus knew His disciples would face situations that would frighten and intimidate them. In this context, He is explaining that following Him will not be an easy path. There will be rejection. There will be hostility. There quite possibly will be death. The world in which He is sending them will not welcome them with open arms.

How were they to respond? They were to go, despite the danger and the obstacles. Jesus gives them full disclosure of the hardships they will face, but He also reassures them that they will not be alone. When the time comes for them to speak, His Spirit will give them the words.

As we follow after Christ, intent on sharing the gospel with those we meet, there will be times when we do not know what to say. It may be a conversation with a person who is not open to hearing the words of truth, or perhaps it is someone who is interested, but has a hundred questions. You may feel ill-equipped; you may think you are in over your head! You may be scared.

Jesus' words reassure us that God's Spirit will give us exactly what we are to say, at just the right time. We must believe this promise. We cannot let our fears or lack of confidence keep us from speaking the gospel, even when we feel we will say all the wrong things. God's Spirit is able to take our words spoken in humility and obedience, and speak them into the heart of the hearer.

Live It Out

Jesus told His disciples, "Do not worry about what you will say." This takes incredible trust! But don't you see how God works? When we are dependent on Him to give us the right words at the right moment, we are forced to be listening! Our relationship with Him deepens, as we stay close, with a pure heart and open eyes and ears, intent on what He is speaking. Our words for others are an overflow of what God has poured into us.

1 Corinthians 2:12-13 (NLT) – *And we have received God's Spirit (not the world's spirit), so we can know the wonderful things God has freely given us. When we tell you these things, we do not use words that come from human wisdom. Instead, we speak words given to us by the Spirit, using the Spirit's words to explain spiritual truths.*

PRAY TODAY:
Dear Jesus, I am unworthy, to be Your messenger. To know that You want me to speak of Your gospel to others is overwhelming, and a great privilege. And while my heart desires to speak it effectively and with great results, I realize that I am completely dependent on You to speak through me. My words are human words, and will not achieve Your salvation. I surrender my mind and heart to You. Fill me with Your words, through Your Spirit. Let my words and my thoughts be Yours, so that You get all the glory. Amen.

Day Eighteen: Spirit-filled = Spirit controlled.

Take It In

Therefore, be careful how you walk not as unwise men but as wise, making the most of your time because the days are evil. So then do not be foolish, but understand what the will of the Lord is. And do not get drunk with wine, for that is dissipation, but be filled with the Spirit. Ephesians 5:15-18

Think It Through

What is the comparison that Paul is trying to make, by using the example of being drunk as opposed to being filled with the Spirit? To answer that question, we must look at the context of the previous two verses. We are instructed to make the most of our time, and to understand God's will.

Realize that the Spirit of God directs our steps. Daily, He is bringing us into contact with individuals upon whom that same Spirit of God has been working, preparing their hearts to hear the gospel. This makes the meaning of these verses clear. We are not to waste our time! The days are evil – surely that is an apt description of our culture. People are living in deception, denying the power of God and illiterate about the Bible. God's heart desire is that men repent and come to salvation. We are not to be distracted, foolish and unwise, wasting our time with things that do not matter, but are to be filled with the Spirit.

To be filled with the Spirit is to be controlled by Him, just as to be drunk is to be controlled by the effects of alcohol. When we are Spirit-filled, we are listening and obeying. We are sensitive to the spiritual condition of others. To be filled with God's Spirit is to have His heart, His desires. It is to be a conduit of His mercy and grace to a dying world.

Live It Out

As a believer, the Spirit of God indwells you. We have all of Him that we will ever need to live a Spirit-led life. The key is surrendering to His control. If we want to be an effective witness, we must learn to listen to the Spirit of God, and obey His promptings.

Romans 8:14 – *For all who are being led by the Spirit of God, these are the sons of God.*

PRAY TODAY:
Dear Jesus, I confess that I am easily distracted, and guilt of wasting my time. My heart's desire is to be filled with your Spirit, controlled by Your desires, listening and obeying. Help me to make the most of my days on earth. Your Word promises that You will be my guide and my helper. I surrender myself again to you today. Amen.

Day Nineteen: The love of the Spirit to love others.

Take It In

And not only this, but we also exult in our tribulations, knowing that tribulation brings about perseverance; and perseverance, proven character; and proven character, hope; and hope does not disappoint, because the love of God has been poured out within our hearts through the Holy Spirit who was given to us. Romans 5:3-5

But I say to you, love your enemies and pray for those who persecute you.
Matthew 5:44

Think It Through

Do you find it hard to love your enemies? Who are your enemies?

According to scripture, those who are a friend of the world (the current culture we live in) is an enemy of God (James 4:4). Since we are the children of God, His enemies are our enemies.

The hardest people to share the gospel with are those who have no use for God and do not see themselves as sinners separated from God. They have no desire for Him. What are we to do? Jesus commands us to **love them** and **pray for them.** Perhaps it is someone you have shared the gospel with, but they rejected you. What is rejection of the gospel, but a rejection of God? We just happen to be the recipient of that rejection.

How does God's Spirit empower us to respond?

Because God's love has been poured out into our hearts, through the indwelling Holy Spirit, we can love those who hate God. We cannot love our enemies, those who need God, in our human flesh. Our flesh will fight for our rights, and our opinions.

Love for our enemies is an overflow of the love we have experienced ourselves.

Love for our enemies comes when we remember that we, too, once were enemies of God, and that someone loved us enough to pray for us.

Live It Out

Who is it in our life that we struggle to love? Who has closed their ears to the gospel, and maybe even mocks us for our faith in God? The answer is not to argue. The answer is to ask God to give us His love for them. As we commit to pray for those who are enemies of God in obedience to Jesus' command, the Spirit of God will fill our heart with a supernatural love that we can't explain. And it is the outpouring of this love into their lives that will cause them to see how much God loves them and believe what He did to save them.

Galatians 5:16 – *But I say, walk by the Spirit, and you will not carry out the desire of the flesh.*

PRAY TODAY:
Dear Jesus, I want to love Your enemies. In my flesh, when I see and hear people say ungodly things about You, things I know are not true, it makes me angry. But I know this is not how You want me to respond. You are patient toward the unrighteous, giving them time to repent, just as You did not destroy me for my sin, but offered me forgiveness. I ask that Your Spirit so fill my mind and heart that my words, thoughts and actions will overflow in love for others, so that they will see You for who You are, and come to know You. Amen.

Day Twenty: Spirit-filled words that give grace.

Take It In

Let no unwholesome word proceed from your mouth, but only such a word as is good for edification according to the need of the moment, so that it will give grace to those who hear. Do not grieve the Holy Spirit of God, by whom you were sealed for the day of redemption.
Ephesians 4:29-30

Think It Through

If you are a parent, you've probably experienced being embarrassed by something your child said. Maybe it was your preschooler who repeats a curse word in front of your pastor – a word they picked up from you in the privacy of your home. Or maybe it was your teenager who expressed a viewpoint you would be shocked for someone else to hear. A viewpoint that would **grieve your heart** if others believed you also felt that way.

I find it very informative that the context of a verse warning us against grieving the Holy Spirit is right after a verse about the words we say. The word **grieve** means to cause distress or sorrow, to offend, to cause pain or grief. What kind of words grieve the Spirit of God? Words that are unwholesome (corrupt, rotten, or worthless). Words that do not edify (build up or encourage) others. Words that do not give grace to those who hear.

Our words have the power to "give grace." Through our conversations, we can bring the grace of God into a situation. We can "minister grace" – give the gift of God's grace, through words that bring pleasure and joy to the Spirit of God. Or, in contrast, we can say things that embarrass Him and cause Him pain.

As we learn to walk in the Spirit, listening and obey as He prompts us to speak and act in ways that reveal the glorious gospel, we must watch our words carefully, that they do not distract or destroy the message we are trying to communicate.

Live It Out

How comfortable are we knowing that God hears every word that we say? If the person we have been praying for and witnessing to were to hear our private conversations, would they find grace in our words? Would our words paint a true picture of the God we publicly proclaim? Our words are powerful, speaking life or death to those around us.

Colossians 4:6 – *Let your speech always be with grace, as though seasoned with salt, so that you will know how you should respond to each person.*

PRAY TODAY:
Dear Jesus, I never want to offend You by my words. I know that in my human flesh, my words can be sharp and ugly. Forgive me when my tongue causes me to sin, and causes You pain and sorrow. I ask that Your Holy Spirit empower my words with the gospel, and with the grace that You desire to lavish on those around me. Let me speak words that represent You, words that will draw others toward the truth. Keep me from conversations and words that would grieve You. Amen.

An Awareness of the People Around Us
Day 21 – Day 25

Go therefore and make disciples of all the nations,
baptizing them in the name of the Father and the Son and the Holy Spirit,
teaching them to observe all that I have commanded you;
and lo, I am with you always, even to the end of the age.
Matthew 28:19-20

Here we have what is commonly referred to as the "Great Commission."
The word "go" means to take a walk, or continue a journey, to traverse.
We can understand Jesus' command in this way:
"As you are going, make disciples!"

As we grow in awareness of the Spirit's leading, we will meet people,
not by accident, but by the sovereignty of God, as directed by His Spirit.
Because we have a new awareness of the lost,
and are walking in an attitude of prayer,
we will begin to recognize these "chance" meetings as opportunities.

We will become aware of the spiritual condition of others, and our
responsibility to speak the gospel into their lives.

Day Twenty-One: The person of peace.

Take It In

And He [Jesus] was saying to them, "The harvest is plentiful, but the laborers are few; therefore beseech the Lord of the harvest to send out laborers into His harvest. Go; behold, I send you out as lambs in the midst of wolves. Carry no money belt, no bag, no shoes; and greet no one on the way. Whatever house you enter, first say, 'Peace be to this house.' If a man of peace is there, your peace will rest on him; but if not, it will return to you." Luke 10:2-6

Think It Through

Jesus introduced the concept of a "man of peace." What does this mean?

As He sent out His disciples to go ahead of Him into the cities where He would soon come, He instructed them to find a home where they would be welcomed. The size of the house, or the influence of the person living there did not matter. They were to look for a place where their message would be received.

How would they find this "man of peace?" They were to speak peace to him, and test his response. To speak peace to someone is to present the message of peace, the gospel. It is to initiate a conversation about spiritual things, to discover their interest in continuing the conversation. Sometimes we do this by sharing our own story of conversion, or making a connection by giving evidence of God's activity in your life, such as an answered prayer or need that God met.

As we spend time with our neighbors, friends, and co-workers we will see the truth of Jesus' words: we are as lambs among wolves. Those who are hostile to the gospel will be easily recognized. While we are instructed to love and pray for them (Matthew 5:44), we are not to try to convince them of their need for the gospel. That is a work to be done by God's Spirit. We are to look for individuals who are open to our words of truth. We are to look for people of peace.

Live It Out

Sometimes a person of peace may be right in front of us, but we are too busy to notice. As God increases our awareness of our responsibility to

40

share the gospel, He will also increase our opportunities. Ask Him to help you notice the friend or co-worker whom He is preparing to hear the gospel. Do they have a need? Ask if you can pray for them. Share your own story. They just might be your person of peace!

Luke 10:16 – *The one who listens to you listens to Me, and the one who rejects you rejects Me; and he who rejects Me rejects the One who sent Me.*

PRAY TODAY:
Dear Jesus, I want to recognize the people around me who are ready to have conversations about You. I confess that I tend to rush through my day, trying to accomplish everything on my "to do" list, and in my busy-ness I miss where You are at work. I don't want to miss You! Slow me down, and make me aware of those around me. Let me not miss the prompting of Your Spirit to speak to someone You are drawing to Yourself. Amen.

Day Twenty-Two: The person that is not ready to hear.

Take It In

They passed through the Phrygian and Galatian region, having been forbidden by the Holy Spirit to speak the word in Asia; and after they came to Mysia, they were trying to go into Bithynia, and the Spirit of Jesus did not permit them; and passing by Mysia, they came down to Troas. A vision appeared to Paul in the night: a man of Macedonia was standing and appealing to him, and saying, "Come over to Macedonia and help us." When he had seen the vision, immediately we sought to go into Macedonia, concluding that God had called us to preach the gospel to them.
Acts 16:6-10

Think It Through

Here we see the Spirit of God giving clear and specific direction to Paul and Timothy. They had a desire to share the gospel in Asia, but were told "no." Then they made their way towards Mysia, but were again stopped by the Spirit. Finally, they were given a vision to go to Macedonia, so they were able to proceed. Why would God stop Paul from going to Asia? Did He not want the Asian people to hear the gospel? Of course He did! God's desire is for all men to come to repentance. But He had a plan and purpose for Paul's life. There were individuals in Macedonia whom God was calling to Himself, and He had chosen Paul to be the one to deliver the life-giving message of the gospel! God was directing Paul's steps, to accomplish His plans.

I believe this illustrates that not everyone is ready to hear the gospel. Perhaps the people in Asia and Mysia had not yet experienced all that was necessary for them to be receptive to the truth. We can all give testimony to lessons that we've learned only because we had life experiences to teach us. We all must come to the end of ourselves, our self-sufficiency, pride, and love of the world, before we are ready to hear the message of a better way. God must allow us to see our need of Him before we are willing to repent and ask for His help.

Walking in the Spirit means listening to God's voice, as He directs our steps towards those who are ready to listen, and keeps us from pushing others farther away from the gospel by preaching a message of hope to a heart that is still too hard to hear. We pray for all to come to Christ, but we speak and act as God opens the door.

Live It Out

Jesus tells a parable about the sower (Christ-follower) and the seed (the Word of God). The seeds fall on the ground, but the ground may not be ready to receive it. The seed will take root, but not before the ground has been cultivated and prepared. Sometimes, our job will just be to pick up the rocks and till the soil. It is the Lord of the harvest who determines who tills the soil, who plows the row, and who sows the seed. As you labor in the field where God has placed you, be willing to serve in whatever capacity the Master desires.

Matthew 13:23 – *And the one on whom seed was sown on the good soil, this is the man who hears the word and understands it; who indeed bears fruit and brings forth, some a hundredfold, some sixty, and some thirty."*

PRAY TODAY:
Dear Jesus, I stand in awe of You, the Lord of the harvest. If we were left to our own wisdom, we would miss those who are ready to hear Your gospel, and alienate those who are not. But Your Spirit gives us insight and direction, so we can be used by You to reap a great harvest of souls. The salvation of men is Your work, and You are drawing hearts to Yourself all around us. I am willing to serve in Your harvest however You need me – let me till the soil of those with hard hearts, and sow the seeds of the gospel in those You have prepared. Amen.

Day Twenty-Three: Seeing the heart as God sees it.

Take It In

Now there was a man at Caesarea named Cornelius, a centurion of what was called the Italian cohort, a devout man and one who feared God with all his household, and gave many alms to the Jewish people and prayed to God continually.
Acts 10:1-2

Think It Through

Reading the description of Cornelius, one would conclude that he was a godly man. He was devout (having a reverent and dutiful attitude toward God), feared God, was generous to those in need, and prayed a lot. Looking at his life from the outside, we would assume that he was a Christian.

God, however, looks at the heart. He saw a desire in Cornelius to know and serve God, but he was missing the central message of salvation: Jesus. To meet the spiritual need of Cornelius, God went to great lengths to bring Peter to Caesarea (read Acts 10 for the details). Cornelius was a religious man, and a good man, but he needed someone to tell him the gospel, the meaning of Jesus' death, burial, and resurrection.

How often do we meet people and make assumptions based on their outward appearance or behavior? We observe that they are a "good" person, are kind and gracious, and do many good things. We assume that they do not need to hear the gospel, or that they have heard it before, and move on towards the more obvious unbeliever.

We should never make assumptions about the spiritual condition of others. A person who is outwardly religious may be as far from the gospel as the unrepentant serial killer on death row. Our enemy, Satan, is a great deceiver, and there are many people who believe their good works are enough to gain them entry into heaven. We should share the gospel with everyone who is willing to hear, and trust God to reveal truth to the heart.

Live It Out

Think about the people who live near you, or work with you. Ask God for divine encounters and conversations that will reveal their true spiritual condition. If they are truly a follower of Christ, they will not be offended that you want to make sure they know Him. And if they have been deceived about what it means to serve and know God, you will know how to pray for them, and how to talk with them more about Jesus.

1 Samuel 16:7 - *But the Lord said to Samuel, "Do not look at his appearance or at the height of his stature, because I have rejected him; for God sees not as man sees, for man looks at the outward appearance, but the Lord looks at the heart."*

PRAY TODAY:
Dear Jesus, I confess that sometimes I put on a good show in front of others, especially those whom I want to believe I am a good person. I can hide what is in my heart from others. In the same way, I realize that I cannot see into the hearts of the people around me. I know many people who have an appearance of godliness, but might not know You personally. Help me not to make judgments of others based on what I can see, but depend on Your wisdom and direction to guide my words and my actions to influence everyone I meet for the gospel. Amen.

Day Twenty-Four: The person God has planned for you to meet.

Take It In

And on the Sabbath day we went outside the gate to a riverside, where we were supposing that there would be a place of prayer; and we sat down and began speaking to the women who had assembled. A woman named Lydia, from the city of Thyatira, a seller of purple fabrics, a worshiper of God, was listening; and the Lord opened her heart to respond to the things spoken by Paul. Acts 16:13-14

Think It Through

The city of Thyatira was located in Asia Minor, on the border of Mysia, exactly the place where the Spirit of God had forbidden Paul to go earlier in this chapter. God had instead directed him towards Macedonia, and plans a divine meeting with a citizen from the very place where Paul had desired to preach! In Revelation 3, we learn that Thyatira was full of false teachers, illustrated by a woman called Jezebel. Isn't it interesting that God arranged for Lydia to be in Philippi at just the right time, to hear Paul's message of the gospel?

Lydia is the perfect picture of the "person of peace" as mentioned by Jesus in Luke 10. She had two great qualities. First, she was a worshiper of God. She was not hostile towards the truth of scripture, but knew in her heart that she was created to worship. When she met Paul, she was not yet a believer, but was open to the message. Secondly, she listened! She desired to hear the truth. She had been exposed to enough false teaching in her city; she had heard enough confusing messages on how to gain favor with God. She was hungry for truth, so she listened.

What was the result? God opened her heart to respond! When a person has a respect for God, and a sincere desire to know truth, God will answer the cry of their heart. We see that Lydia truly accepted salvation, for her immediate action was to be baptized, and to invite Paul and his team of missionaries into the house where she was staying, so she could learn more.

God honored Paul's desire to preach the gospel to Asia Minor and Mysia. It was not His plan for Paul to go to them, so He brought a citizen of that area right into Paul's sphere of influence. And it was not just any citizen – it was a woman who was hungry to hear truth, and who was ready to respond to God's invitation.

Live It Out

Perhaps you have a desire to serve God in a place where He has not yet opened the door. Obey God by allowing Him to use you where He has planted you but don't be surprised when He satisfies the desire of your heart in a completely unexpected way! Maybe you have a heart for the unsaved in foreign countries. Why not ask God to show you how to meet individuals from that country right in your own neighborhood or city? There may be places to volunteer in your community where you can minister in a strategic way. And while you are there, be prepared to share your story with the people you meet who are hungry for truth and whose hearts are ready to respond.

1 Peter 4:10-11 – *As each one has received a special gift, employ it in serving one another as good stewards of the grace of the manifold grace of God. Whoever speaks, is to do so as one who is speaking the utterances of God; who-ever serves is to do so as one who is serving by the strength which God supplies.*

PRAY TODAY:
Dear Jesus, I thank You that You always have a plan. Sometimes I think of great ideas, but they may not be Your ideas. You are not only working in my life, but in the lives of the people around me, and you are ordering my steps so that I can be of use to You, and available to share Your story to those You will bring into my life – those who are ready to respond to You. Use me whenever and wherever You see fit. Amen.

Day Twenty-Five: Opportunities with outsiders.

Take It In

Conduct yourselves with wisdom toward outsiders, making the most of the opportunity.
Colossians 4:5

Think It Through

Have you ever been an "outsider?" The dictionary defines it as *a person who does not belong.* We've all experienced this at some stage of life – maybe in middle school (where it seems no one really fits in), or perhaps in a job, where you were the only Christian in the office. You feel awkward and unaccepted. As believers, we are called "aliens" and "sojourners" because we know that this world is not our home; our citizenship is in heaven.

In Colossians 4:5, however, we see that the real outsiders are those who are not a part of God's family. The King James reads: *those who are without.* We could say, "without what?" Without salvation. Without hope. Without Jesus. While we may *feel* like an outsider, consider what it means to actually *be* one!

We are told to conduct ourselves with wisdom toward outsiders. Acting wisely includes the words of our mouth, the attitudes of our heart, as well as our actions. When we are around those do not believe in God, we should consciously be speaking and acting in ways that draws others towards Christ. We must realize that we may only have one opportunity to leave an impression about who Jesus is. We should be sensitive to what others think and believe and never give them a reason to reject Christ based on our behavior.

Live It Out

Think for a moment what it feels like to be an outsider. Now take that feeling and turn it into compassion for the person who does not know Christ. What words can you speak that will encourage them to consider Him? What actions can you take that will cause them to reflect on the truth? How can you illustrate with your attitudes and actions that God loves them and desires them?

Colossians 4:6 – *Let your speech always be with grace, as though seasoned with salt, so that you will know how you should respond to each person.*

PRAY TODAY
Dear Jesus, I ask You to set a guard over my mouth! I ask that Your Spirit convict me when my actions or attitudes towards those who do not know you, those who are outside salvation, might push them away from You, or misrepresent You. Help me to take advantage of every opportunity to be a witness for the gospel, and to speak and act in ways that reflect Your love, Your goodness, Your mercy and Your grace. And help me not to forget that I once was an outsider too, until someone showed my Your love. Amen.

An Awareness to Love and Serve
Day 26 – Day 32

Let us hold fast the confession of our hope without wavering,
for He who promised is faithful; and let us consider how to stimulate one
another to love and good deeds.
Hebrews 10:23-24

For even the Son of Man did not come to be served, but to serve,
and to give His life a ransom for many.
Mark 10:45

Growing in spiritual awareness means that you are going to
notice the needs of others. It's impossible to pray for
someone and not experience a growing love for them.
Along with that comes a desire to help them, to meet their physical and
spiritual needs.

Jesus did not come to our world to be served, but gave us the greatest
example of a servant's heart. He lay down His very life for us.

As we seek to fulfill the mission of sharing Christ with our neighbors,
co-workers and friends, we will discover the way to their heart is
through good deeds of service and love.

Day Twenty-Six: Loving others means being truthful.

Take It In

Therefore I, the prisoner of the Lord, implore you to walk in a manner worthy of the calling with which you have been called, with all humility and gentleness with patience, showing tolerance for one another in love.
Ephesians 4:1-2

Think It Through

"Showing tolerance for one another in love."

In today's political and cultural climate, we are told repeatedly and continually that we are to be tolerant of one another, that we are to love each other. This is, in fact, a biblical principle, as we see here. The problem is that humans instinctively lean toward the extreme, and we like to take one phrase out of context and make it our mantra, excluding the rest of scripture (and usually common sense as well).

Does 'showing tolerance' mean that it is wrong to expose sin? Is it "intolerant" to share with an unbeliever that their choices in life are wrong and sinful, according to God's word?

Let me ask you a question. If you saw a person sitting in the middle of the train tracks having a picnic lunch with their family, with no awareness that there was a speeding train fast approaching, what would you say? Would you think, "Well, it's their right to eat lunch wherever they want. Who am I to judge where they choose to sit?" Of course not! Neither would we say, "I am so angry that they are choosing to sit on the tracks! I would never do such a foolish thing. They are getting what they deserve!" Nor would we think, "I don't want to say anything or go around them, because then I might be tempted to sit on the tracks too."

Instead, we would cry out to them. We would beg them to get off the tracks. We would tell them of the danger that is coming their way. We would offer to help them up and carry their children to safety.

Sin separates men from God.
Sin leads to death.
Sin brings pain and suffering.

Sin causes heartache and broken relationships.
Sin is the enemy of mankind.
Sin keeps men out of heaven, and sends them to hell.

Live It Out

Read again the phrase: *showing tolerance to one another in love.* Nowhere in scripture are we told to "tolerate" sin by renaming it, ignoring it, or covering it up. But we are told to **tolerate one another.** Have you been guilty of tolerating sin for the sake of political correctness, because you are afraid to offend someone, or because you think it is unkind to speak the truth? If so, you must ask yourself if you really understand the cost of sin. The reality is that people who do not repent will spend eternity separated from God. Are you willing to risk telling someone the truth?

Ephesians 5:5 – *For this you know with certainty, that no immoral or impure person or covetous man, who is an idolater, has an inheritance in the kingdom of Christ and God.*

PRAY TODAY
Dear Jesus, Forgive me for thinking so little of sin. I confess that I often forget the magnitude of what it cost You. Convict me and show me where I have let culture tell me how to respond to sin. Help me to understand that really loving someone means telling them the truth about sin, and the good news that You came to rescue us from it, because You truly loved us. Amen.

Day Twenty-Seven: Love means being humble and gentle.

Take It In

But speaking the truth in love, we are to grow up in all aspects into Him who is the Head, even Christ. ... Therefore, laying aside falsehood, speak truth each one of you with his neighbor, for we are members of one another. Ephesians 4:15,25

Think It Through

Paul's letter to the church at Ephesus is written to believers. He is teaching us how to live with one another in a way that glorifies God. The command is for Christ-followers to tell each other the truth, in a way that shows we love one another. I believe this same principle applies when speaking to unbelievers. We are to tell them the truth, in a way that expresses how much God loves them.

Yesterday we spoke of tolerance. The word in the Greek is *anechōi* and actually means to sustain, to bear up, or to endure. It is a verb. Tolerance is not an attitude, it is an action. It is not simply "putting up with" someone else in spite of our differences. It is an active word, implying to suffer, or forbear.

True tolerance is loving someone while being willing to tell them the truth. It is standing firm against sin, while speaking and acting in love. We tolerate people, even when they are hateful toward us. We see beyond their words and actions and love the soul of the person, because we too, once, were intolerant and wicked. We expose sin, not because we think we are better than someone else, but because we know that the truth is the only remedy, the only hope.

Tolerance means we are willing to be ridiculed and seen as foolish, so that God's mercy and grace can work through us. We stand firm on scripture's definition of sin, while serving and loving the sinner.

Ephesians 4:2 tells us **how** we are to show tolerance: with **humility, gentleness and patience.** We are humble, because we know that we, too, were once sinners. We are gentle, because we are dealing with wounded hearts. And we are patient, just as God was patient with us, giving us time to repent and come to the light.

Live It Out

Lest you get the wrong idea, let me be clear. We are not called to be "spiritual hall monitors" pointing out the sin in everyone's life around us. We are called to live and speak about the gospel. But as God brings us into relationships with people, we must not compromise on sin in order to "keep the door open." A false gospel says you can come to Christ and stay in your sin. This is a lie. We must present the whole gospel – our sinful life in exchange for Christ's righteousness.

Tell the truth, but tell it in love.
Tell it with humility, gentleness and patience, just as Jesus would.
Because aren't you glad someone told you?

Ephesians 5:6 – *Let no one deceive you with empty words, for because of these things the wrath of God comes upon the sons of disobedience.*

PRAY TODAY
Dear Jesus, Thank You for sending someone into my life that told me the truth. I know how devastating sin can be, and I never want to leave someone with the idea that sin is acceptable and that we can come to You and still hold onto our old ways of sin. Help me to be bold enough to share the truth with the people You bring into my life, and show me how to communicate in love and humility. Let me truly love others by telling them the truth.
Amen.

Day Twenty-Eight: The purpose of good deeds.

Take It In

Keep your behavior excellent among the Gentiles, so that in the thing in which they slander you as evildoers, they may because of your good deeds, as they observe them, glorify God in the day of visitation.
1 Peter 2:12

Think It Through

The world typically thinks of "good deeds" or "good works" as something we do to make God (or the gods) happy. They believe that in order for God to approve of them, they must do things for Him. If a person does a lot of "good works," then it will balance (cancel out) their bad decisions and sinful choices, and they will gain rewards in heaven. Even a believer can fall into the false idea that good works are a way to gain the approval of our Father.

But scripture teaches a different concept. Good deeds have far more to do with our character, our inner spiritual man, than our outward actions. In the verse above, we see that "behavior" is equated to "good deeds." Good deeds are simply an overflow of a heart that is surrendered to God in obedience, trust, and gratitude. We choose to speak and act in ways that bring glory to God. A person who does not know God can do good things, and accomplish many good works, but their works do not earn them the favor with God they seek. A biblical good deed brings attention and glory to God. Biblical good deeds – godly character – is a response from a regenerated heart. Worldly good works are an attempt to justify oneself before God.

The Bible commands us to engage in good deeds for several reasons. One primary reason is that the world is watching. As we engage unbelievers with a godly character and commitment to serving them through good deeds, they will observe our actions, and will see in them a reason to glorify God. The reverse is true: our poor choices, our "ungodly deeds" observed by those who are lost, will cause them to lose respect for God, and to doubt the truth of scripture. Our faith will appear empty and ineffective.

Live It Out

What is the motivation behind the good things you do? Is it to gain God's approval? Is it to appear spiritual to others? Or is it simply to act and speak in ways that cause others to consider the Savior? Perhaps you need to consider what it is in your life that is bringing negative attention toward God? Ask God to search your heart and mind for any habits, actions or attitudes that would cause an unbeliever to turn away from Him. Confess it, and determine to use your influence to bring glory and attention to God.

Titus 2:7-8 – *In all things show yourself to be an example of good deeds, with purity in doctrine, dignified, sound in speech which is beyond reproach, so that the opponent will be put to shame, having nothing bad to say about us.*

PRAY TODAY
Dear Jesus, I recognize that all of my good works are nothing unless they are from a heart that desires to love and serve You, and bring attention to Your name. Anything I do in my own strength and from my own motivations will be human, earthly, and simply be an empty offering. But as I surrender myself to You, You can take the time and resources and talents that You have given me and use them for Your glory, and to draw others to Yourself. Keep me from anything that would distract others from seeing Your glory. Amen.

Day Twenty-Nine: Spending our life on things that really matter.

Take It In

For the grace of God has appeared, bringing salvation to all men, instructing us to deny ungodliness and worldly desires and to live sensibly, righteously and godly in the present age, looking for the blessed hope and the appearing of the glory of our great God and Savior, Christ Jesus, who gave Himself for us to redeem us from every lawless deed, and to purify for Himself a people for His own possession, zealous for good deeds.
Titus 2:11-14

Think It Through

This passage of scripture is a wonderful summary of what the Christian's life should be after salvation! It simplifies life, and if taken to heart and lived out, brings a clarity of purpose and a confidence that we are doing exactly what God has called us to do! Consider the four key elements we find here:

Deny ungodliness and worldly desires.
Stay away from sin and say no to what your flesh wants. Avoid anything that brings shame to God.

Live sensibly, righteously and godly in the present age.
Commit to being "anti-culture." The world we live in hates Jesus. Expect it. Make life choices that honor God.

Keep looking up, expecting Jesus to return at any moment.
It could happen today. The hope of Jesus' return keeps us from being distracted or discouraged.

Do good things with a passion that comes from knowing you belong to God.
You only have so much energy, passion and zeal. Spend it on things that really matter: good deeds that serve others, love others, and cause others to want what we have: salvation and a relationship with God.

Live It Out

Life can quickly get complicated and chaotic. Our enemy is the master of distraction, and the daily routines of work, school, career, parenting, marriage, etc. can steal our joy and keep us from doing what really matters. We are on this earth for one purpose: to be changed into the image of Christ and to tell others how He has transformed us. What one thing can you eliminate from your life today, that will better allow you to carry out that purpose? Let's keep our hearts and lives free from sin, live righteously and be zealous for good deeds that influence others for the gospel…because He's coming soon!

Philippians 3:13-14 – *Brethren, I do not regard myself as having laid hold of it yet; but one thing I do; forgetting what lies behind and reaching forward to what lies ahead, I press on toward the goal for the prize of the upward call of God in Christ Jesus.*

PRAY TODAY
Dear Jesus, I am thankful that You never intended life to be complicated. I confess that I get caught up in all of the things that my day-to-day life demands of me. My world is busy, and my tendency is to be distracted by things that do not matter, and miss the most important things. Forgive me for making life harder than it needs to be. Thank You for Your word, that gives me perspective, settles my heart, and fills me with Your peace. Teach me how to order my days so that I can be zealous and passionate for what brings You glory. Amen.

Day Thirty: Don't lose heart.

Take It In

For you were called to freedom, brethren; only do not turn your freedom into an opportunity for the flesh, but through love serve one another. For the whole Law is fulfilled in one word, in the statement, "You shall love your neighbor as yourself."
Galatians 5:13-14

Let us not lose heart in doing good, for in due time we will reap if we do not grow weary. So then, while we have opportunity, let us do good to all people, and especially to those who are of the household of the faith.
Galatians 6:9-10

Think It Through

Have you ever heard the phrase, "pay it forward?" The phrase may have been coined by Lily Hardy Hammond in her 1916 book *In the Garden of Delight*, in which she states, "You don't pay love back. You pay it forward." The concept is used in financial transactions, in which a creditor offers a debtor the option of paying the debt forward, by lending to a third person instead of paying the original creditor back.

This is a beautiful picture of the gospel. God so loved us that He gave us His only Son (John 3:16). We can never repay this kind of love, and God doesn't ask us to. He simply asks us to "pay it forward" to the people around us, both believers and non-believers. We are to "love our enemies" (Matthew 5:44), "love our neighbor" (Romans 13:8) and "love other believers" (1 Peter 1:22). Yes, we must love God first and best (Matthew 5:43), and as we draw from the well of His heart, His love spills over in good deeds and service to our family, our friends, our co-workers, and our neighbors. What greater way could there be to repay the debt that God paid in full on our account, than to love others as He loves us?

Love is an action, and it is a decision of the will. It is living intentionally, speaking, acting, serving, and giving to others. We do good things for our brothers and sisters in Christ to encourage them. We do good things for unbelievers so that they will see the love of Christ in us. We serve, because Christ served us, by coming to earth to live, die and be raised for our justification.

Live It Out

Consider the encouraging words of Galatians 6:9: *Let us not lose heart in doing good.* Do you ever feel that no matter what you do, no matter how many kind acts of service, or gentle words you speak, that your neighbor will never respond to the gospel? Are you ever discouraged that you have prayed for years for someone to be saved, with no results?

Don't give up. Keep on praying. Keep on serving. Keep on loving. We never know how God is working in someone – we only see the outside, but God sees the heart. Keep paying the love of God forward into the hearts and homes of the people with whom you live, work and play. *In due time, we will reap if we do not grow weary.*

1 Thessalonians 2:7-8 – *But we proved to be gentle among you, as a nursing mother tenderly cares for her own children. Having so fond an affection for you, we were well-pleased to impart to you not only the gospel of God but also our own lives, because you had become very dear to us.*

PRAY TODAY
Dear Jesus, I am amazed at how You love me. You came to this earth to pay my sin debt, and set me free. You rescued me, and transferred me to Your kingdom. I owe You my life, and a debt I can never pay. Thank You that I can demonstrate in some small way how much I love You by loving others – those who love me back and those who hate me. I ask that today Your Spirit will show me how I can serve and love those who do not know You, so that they have just a small taste of the love that You have poured into my heart. Amen.

Day Thirty-One: Loving others by showing mercy.

Take It In

And a lawyer stood up and put Him to the test, saying, "Teacher, what shall I do to inherit eternal life?" And He said to him, "What is written in the Law? How does it read to you?" And he answered, "You shall love the Lord your God with all your heart, and with all your soul, and with all your strength, and with all your mind; and your neighbor as yourself." And He said to him, "You have answered correctly; do this and you will live." But wishing to justify himself, he said to Jesus, "And who is my neighbor?" ... [Jesus asked] "Which of these three do you think proved to be a neighbor to the man who fell into the robbers' hands?" And [the lawyer] said, "The one who showed mercy toward him." Then Jesus said to him, "Go and do the same."
Luke 10:25-29, 36-37

Think It Through

How could Jesus tell a lawyer that loving God and loving our neighbor would result in eternal life? Isn't that salvation by works? Doesn't that sound like we can earn God's favor? We know from other scriptures (Ephesians 2:8-9 for example) that salvation is a gift, unearned and undeserved, and comes only by faith through grace.

The key is understanding that **Jesus knows the condition of our heart.** It is impossible for us to love God with all that we are, our heart, soul, strength and mind, unless we first experience the love of God poured into us by the Holy Spirit. It is only after salvation comes to us through faith and true repentance that we are able to love God, and in turn, love our neighbors.

We love, because He first loved us. (1 John 4:19)

How do we love our neighbor? By showing mercy, just as the parable of the Good Samaritan teaches us. And the mercy shown is not the means to obtain eternal life...it is the evidence that we are already partakers of it! The one who has experienced mercy, who has tasted the grace of God in forgiveness, is the one who will be first in line to extend mercy to others.

Live It Out

How do we show mercy? The Hebrew word is *eleos* and means *kindness or good will towards the miserable and the afflicted, joined with a desire to help them.* Of all the people you know, who are the most miserable? Who are the afflicted? It is those who are without Christ! While scripture certainly commands us to address the physical poverty in our world, we must see the spiritually destitute as the greatest need. One day, someone showed you mercy by sharing the good news of how you could obtain eternal life through faith in Jesus. As we love God truly and deeply with all of our being, that love will spill over to our neighbors. Who will you show mercy to, today? How will you share God's love?

1 John 3:16-17 – *We know love by this, that He laid down His life for us; and we ought to lay down our lives for the brethren. But whoever has the world's goods, and sees his brother in need and closes his heart against him, how does the love of God abide in him?*

PRAY TODAY
Dear Jesus, Thank You for showing me mercy. When I was rebellious, ungrateful and sinful, You offered grace and forgiveness. You drew me to Yourself, opened my spiritual eyes, and granted me repentance. Thank You for sending someone to demonstrate mercy to me when I was miserable and afflicted. Let me love You completely so that Your love spills over in mercy to those who are spiritually destitute and lost. Amen.

Day Thirty-Two: Encouragement and accountability in serving.

Take It In

Let us hold fast the confession of our hope without wavering, for He who promised is faithful; and let us consider how to stimulate one another to love and good deeds, not forsaking our own assembling together, as is the habit of some, but encouraging one another; and all the more as you see the day drawing near.
Hebrews 10:23-25

Think It Through

The writer of Hebrews challenges us to do two things, because of God's faithfulness to us, and in light of the decaying culture around us.

Hold fast our confession without wavering. What is our confession? It is the profession of our faith: our confession *of* Christ, and *to* Christ. It is to stand firm on what we have professed to believe. It is to be unmoved by our trials, our temptations, and unbending toward those who would press against us, or try to quiet our message. It is to set our roots down deep into the truth of the gospel, and never waver.

Stimulate one another to love and good deeds. The word "stimulate" means to spur, to incite, to provoke or to irritate. Here is a biblical reason to irritate one another (in love)! Whatever it takes, we are to encourage one another to remain focused and faithful on our mission of loving and serving one another and those outside the body of Christ so that they will hear the gospel.

All of us need encouragement and accountability. We are easily distracted and often discouraged. Each one of us is susceptible to being pulled away from the body of Christ. As you commit to intentionally and persistently be a messenger of the gospel where you live, work and play, recognize that our enemy will not be pleased. We need each other, as we hold fast to the faith, and spur one another on.

Live It Out

What is the "day" drawing near that this verse references? It is simply a reminder that one day we will all give account of our lives to God. There is a day of judgment coming. Believers will be held accountable for the work God has called us to do, and there will be rewards, and loss of rewards. Sadly, unbelievers will be held accountable for their sin, resulting in eternal separation from God. Let's not let anyone we know face that day unprepared! Encourage your fellow Christ-followers to be faithful, as we proclaim to a lost world what we profess to believe.

Romans 14:11b-12 – *For we will all stand before the judgment seat of God. For it is written, "As I live," says the Lord, "every knee shall bow to Me, and every tongue shall give praise to God." So then each one of us will give an account of himself to God.*

PRAY TODAY
Dear Jesus, I confess that I sometimes forget that there will be a day of accounting. Because You have poured out Your grace on my life, my human tendency is to grow complacent. Forgive me for taking it for granted. Thank You for putting brothers and sisters in my life who spur me on to be faithful and committed to You and to the work You have given me to do. Help me to be that person for others, and to always be conscious that those who do not know You will be held accountable for their sin. Let that fact remind me to hold fast to my confession of faith, and to proclaim it without wavering so that others will hear. Amen.

An Awareness of the Cross
Day 33 – Day 40

Now I make known to you, brethren, the gospel which I preached to you,
which also you received, in which also you stand,
by which also you are saved if you hold fast the word which I preached to
you, unless you believed in vain.
For I delivered to you as of first importance what I also received,
that Christ died for our sins according to the Scriptures,
and that He was buried,
and that He was raised on the third day according to the Scriptures.
1 Corinthians 15:1-5

It is easy to get caught up in a movement. We love challenges.
We love to accomplish tasks, and we are fulfilled by reaching a goal.
As we learn to walk in a new awareness of the work God desires to do
through us, we must be careful not to focus on the task of our mission
more than the meaning and message of the cross.

For the next eight days, we will focus on Jesus' last week
leading up to His death, burial and resurrection.
Without the cross, we have no mission.
Without the cross, there is no message to share with our unbelieving
friends. Our minds and hearts must always come back to the cross,
remembering what Christ did for us, and why we need a Savior.
It is our own personal encounter at the cross that fuels our passion to
carry the gospel message to the lost.

Day Thirty-Three: Preparing the way for Jesus.

Take It In

This took place to fulfill what was spoken through the prophet; "Say to the daughter of Zion, 'Behold your King is coming to you, gentle and mounted on a donkey, even on a colt, the foal of a beast of burden.'"
Matthew 21:4-5

Go through, go through the gates, clear the way for the people; build up, build up the highway, remove the stones, lift up a standard over the peoples. Behold, the Lord has proclaimed to the end of the earth, say to the daughter of Zion, "Lo, your salvation comes; behold His reward is with Him, and His recompense before Him."
Isaiah 62:10-11

Think It Through

The New Testament writers clearly knew that Jesus' entrance into Jerusalem the weekend before His crucifixion was a fulfillment of Old Testament prophecy. Specifically, we reference Zechariah 9:9 as quoted by the gospel writers, but Isaiah also gives us a prophetic look at the triumphal entry: *Lo, your salvation comes!*

I love this picture of Jesus. He is King of kings, the One who created the universe and all that it contains, yet He humbles Himself to ride into this city He loves on a young donkey, carried along by the excitement and zeal of His own people welcoming and honoring Him. Knowing these same crowds will call out for His execution in just five short days, He fulfills prophecy. The Jewish crowds unknowingly affirm that He indeed is the Son of God, the Messiah.

As Isaiah spoke prophetically of Jesus, consider his words just prior to announcing the coming Savior. He sees salvation coming, but the way must be prepared for the people to receive it. He urges, *Go through the gates! Clear the way for the people! Build up the highway! Remove the stones! Lift a standard over the peoples!* This chapter speaks of God's desire to bless His people. He longs to restore them, to remove their desolation and unrighteousness, and to place them as a crown of beauty in the hand of the Lord. He longs to rejoice over them as a bridegroom rejoices over the bride (Isaiah 62:5).

How can we prepare the way for salvation to come to those whom God longs for?

We **go through the gates**, as we enter our neighborhoods and workplaces – our places of influence. We **clear the way** for people to recognize Jesus, as we live and speak and act like Him. We **build up the highway** for Jesus to ride into their lives, by loving them, serving them, and caring for them. We **remove the stones** by speaking truth, dispelling false beliefs, and sharing our own story of redemption. And we **lift up a standard** by praying for them, raising a spiritual signal for God to move on their behalf.

Live It Out

Ask God to give you a visual of Jesus riding into your neighborhood or community. He comes, bringing salvation. Are the people who live and work around you ready to receive Him? Will you prepare the way?

Zechariah 9:9 - *Rejoice greatly, O daughter of Zion! Shout in triumph, O daughter of Jerusalem! Behold, your king is coming to you; He is just and endowed with salvation, Humble, and mounted on a donkey, Even on a colt, the foal of a donkey.*

PRAY TODAY:
Dear Jesus, I rejoice that you came to me, bringing salvation. I recognize you as the Messiah, the One who came in the name of the Lord. Let me be a person who clears the way for others to recognize you, and to receive the salvation that you bring. Amen.

Day Thirty-Four: Worshipping Jesus.

Take It In

So they made Him a supper there, and Martha was serving; but Lazarus was one of those reclining at the table with Him. Mary then took a pound of very costly perfume of pure nard, and anointed the feet of Jesus and wiped His feet with her hair; and the house was filled with the fragrance of the perfume.
John 12:2-3

Think It Through

The story of Mary's extravagant gift is a familiar one to most of us. In this brief passage (John 12:1-8), John focuses on her actions, and the selfish reaction of Judas as the central teaching. But in focusing only on Mary, we might miss the simple beauty of what was taking place as Jesus ate supper with His friends.

Lazarus...a new man in all respects! Just one chapter prior we read that he had fallen ill, died, was buried, and then brought back to life by Jesus. Sit down next to Lazarus and imagine the conversation he was enjoying with Jesus. It's not far-fetched to think that he had met Abraham, Moses, David and Elijah (just to name a few), while waiting in Paradise (Luke 16), until Jesus called him back to this world! Lazarus would be perfectly at peace, completely secure in the knowledge that Jesus was who He claimed to be. Time was no longer important to Lazarus as he now knew that eternal life was one breath away, just a door to walk through.

Lazarus worshipped Jesus...as he reclined next to Him, sharing a simple meal and conversation.

Martha...busy as ever serving the meal. She'd cried as Lazarus was buried, expressed her frustration and impatience with Jesus' delay. She was Type A, a fixer. Yet as she served Jesus this meal, there was a quiet confidence and assurance. She wasn't rushed or overwhelmed, sensing that her time with Jesus was drawing to a close. She rested in what she could offer Jesus, no longer concerned about Mary's role. The meal was an offering, a tangible gift that she could set before her Creator to show her love and devotion.

Martha worshipped Jesus... as she embraced her gifts, and used them to meet a practical need.

And Mary...always the one at the feet of Jesus. Devoted. Passionate. From the very beginning she seemed to know that Jesus was the Messiah, and her role was simply to worship and to learn. As she realized the end of this extraordinary earthly friendship was coming to a close, she took the most valuable possession she owned and poured it out on Him. Can you sense the room grow quiet as the fragrance filled the room? Can you see the heads turning to see her act of devotion? Can you hear her weeping quietly?

Mary worshipped Jesus...as she shared her most valuable possession to demonstrate her love and devotion.

Lazarus worshipped by spending time with Jesus.
Martha worshipped by serving Jesus.
Mary worshipped by sacrificing for Jesus.

Live It Out

How do you worship Jesus? Each one of us, if we have placed our faith in Jesus, has a different relationship with Him. He has met us at our point of need, and assured our hearts that He is the Messiah, the promised One, our salvation. As we spend this week focused on the incredible act of love represented by the cross, reflect on how He has touched your heart and changed you. You were created for intimacy with Him, to serve Him, to love Him, to spend time with Him. Whatever that looks like for you, however He has made you to worship Him, enjoy that this week. Worship Him.

Psalm 132:7 - *Let us go into His dwelling place; Let us worship at His footstool.*

PRAY TODAY
Dear Jesus, We worship You. We take all that we are, all that You have made us to be and to do, and pour it out on You. May our homes, our workplaces and our communities be filled with the sweet fragrance of Your presence in us, as we worship You with our lives. Amen.

Day Thirty-Five: Serving like Jesus.

Take It In

Now before the Feast of the Passover, Jesus knowing that His hour had come that He would depart out of this world to the Father, having loved His own who were in the world, He loved them to the end. ... [Jesus] got up from supper, and laid aside His garments; and taking a towel, He girded Himself. Then He poured water into the basin, and began to wash the disciples' feet and to wipe them with the towel with which He was girded.
John 13:1,4-5

If I then, the Lord and the Teacher, washed your feet, you also ought to wash one another's feet. For I gave you an example that you also should do as I did to you.
John 13:14-15

Think It Through

I find it interesting that of the four gospels, only John tells us that Jesus washed His disciples' feet. Perhaps because of all the disciples, he was the one who understood that Jesus truly loved him. He refers to himself multiple times as "the disciple whom Jesus loved." John puts the humble act of Jesus washing the dusty feet of His friends in context with this statement: "He loved them to the end" (John 13:1). His time of physically walking and talking with them, teaching them parables, healing the sick, and explaining the kingdom of heaven, was coming to an end. Within hours, their lives would never be the same. So Jesus chose to do something that would make a lasting impression on their mind and heart.

You know this, but the duty of washing feet belonged to the lowest servant in the household. It is an act of humility and servanthood. In taking this role, Jesus exemplified servant-leadership at its best. Jesus is God-incarnate, Creator of all that exists, the Son of the Most High God. In the same way that He had chosen to lay aside His glory and come to earth in human form, He now lays aside His outer garment, kneels in front of this group of rough, selfish men and does the unthinkable – He washes their feet. The last lesson He wanted them to hear and see: *Humble yourself before one another, just as I have humbled Myself for you.*

It's humbling to wash someone's feet, but in our culture, it's often even more humbling to have someone wash your feet. We feel awkward and self-conscious. Feet are not the most beautiful parts of our body. They are often rough and calloused. We fear they might smell, or offend someone. Maybe Jesus was teaching us two lessons in one. In order to let others know how much we love them, we must be willing to serve them humbly, but we must also humble ourselves to be served.

Live It Out

The last verse in this passage, at first glance, seems rather out of place. *"Truly, truly, I say to you, he who receives whomever I send receives Me; and he who receives Me receives Him who sent Me"* (John 13:20). We know that we are "sent" by Jesus to a lost world, to proclaim the gospel. And we are "sent" by Jesus to other believers to encourage one another.

Perhaps the real lesson is that "being sent" and "washing feet" is the same mission. We are to go in humility. We are to go willing to serve. And we are to go on loving them to the end.

PRAY TODAY
Dear Jesus, Thank You for the example You gave by washing the disciples' feet. Your actions convict me, when I am selfish and prideful, and unwilling to do the hard, unpleasant or unappreciated things. Help me to be Your willing servant. I want to love others the way You loved me, and I know that it will cost me my pride. As I ponder what You have done for me, let me be willing to do whatever it takes for others to know You. Amen.

Day Thirty-Six: The peace of Jesus.

Take It In

Do not let your heart be troubled; believe in God, believe also in Me.
John 14:1

Peace I leave with you; My peace I give to you; not as the world gives do I give to you. Do not let your heart be troubled, nor let it be fearful.
John 14:27

Think It Through

These words of Jesus, spoken just hours before He would be arrested and crucified, speak of His concern and love for the disciples, and also His care of us – the ones who would believe. They also show that He knows just how the human heart operates!

What does it mean to have a troubled heart? The word means "to agitate, to cause one inward commotion, to take away calmness of mind, make restless, to render anxious or distressed." It can mean "to strike one's spirit with fear or dread." A troubled heart is that inner conflict, often a physical sensation, that causes us to doubt and fear.

We live in a troubling world. Our culture is accelerating in its decline, sinking farther and farther into immorality and depravity. The line between good and evil, right and wrong is blurred. We wonder how we will be able to teach our children and grandchildren what is true. We wonder what is ahead for our nation and our world.

What is the antidote to a troubled heart? *Believe in God. Believe in Jesus.*

Did you know that Jesus experienced His own troubled heart, so that we could trade ours for His peace? He says in John 12:27, *"Now My soul has become troubled; and what shall I say, 'Father, save Me from this hour?'* **But for this purpose I came to this hour**. *Father, glorify Your name."* Jesus' work – His mission – His purpose in coming, purchased our peace. Peace with God, and the peace of God for this troubling world. The key to accessing that peace? **Believe.**

Live It Out

Are you troubled? Fearful? Anxious? Depressed? Experiencing the peace of God is a matter of faith. It's choosing to believe that His word is true, that He is who He says He is. After Jesus' death, burial, and resurrection, the disciples still had to be reminded. Jesus stood before them in a resurrected, glorified human body, and they still doubted. They were still troubled. What does Jesus have to do for you, before you will believe, and experience the peace He offers?

As believers, we have the answer to the world's troubles. Let's act like we truly believe the message of the Resurrection. Let's live a life of bold and confident faith in a risen Savior, so that the world around us will see and experience the peace He offers.

Luke 24:36-38 – *And while they were telling these things, He Himself stood in their midst and said to them, "Peace be to you." But they were startled and frightened and thought that they were seeing a spirit. And He said to them, "Why are you troubled, and why do doubts arise in your hearts?"*

PRAY TODAY
Dear Jesus, I believe. I believe Your word is true. I believe You are the Son of God, who came to this world to live a perfect, sinless life and die on that cross for me. Because I believe, You have saved me and accepted me as Your own. Forgive me when I allow this world to trouble my heart and lose the peace that You died to give me. Today, I want to walk in the confidence and peace that comes from knowing You are in control. Amen.

Day Thirty-Seven: The prayer of Jesus.

Take It In

And being in agony He was praying very fervently; and His sweat became like drops of blood, falling down upon the ground.
Luke 22:44

As you sent Me into the world, I also have sent them into the world. For their sakes I sanctify Myself, that they themselves also may be sanctified in truth. I do not ask on behalf of these alone, but for those also who believe in Me through their word.
John 17:18-20

Think It Through

Sometimes when we read about the Garden of Gethsemane, where Jesus prayed on the night before He was crucified, we think that His agony in prayer was only for Himself. After all, He prayed, *"Father, if you are willing, remove this cup from Me; yet not My will, but Yours be done."* (Luke 22:42). But John 17 gives a glimpse of what else was on Jesus' mind, other than His imminent death: **you.**

Jesus prayed specific things for His disciples. He asked His Father to give them joy, protection from the enemy, and to set them apart as holy, even as they lived in the world but not of it. He commissioned them, sending them into the world to proclaim what He had taught them about the kingdom of God. And after praying for them, He expands that prayer to include every believer who would come to know the true and living God because of the testimony of those first disciples – and that means **you** and **me.**

What does it mean to you that Jesus had you in mind on the last night before His crucifixion?

It tells me He could see beyond the physical pain and suffering that He faced. He saw the other side of the grave. He saw hope, and life, and peace, and joy. **He saw what His obedience to the cross would gain for the ones who would believe.** He saw the great multitude, people from every tribe and tongue and language, worshipping before the throne in heaven. He saw the end result of the gospel.

Live It Out

There are two lessons to see here. First, the fact that Jesus overcame death gives us hope that no matter what trial or tribulation or challenge we are facing in this life, there is a resurrection on the other side. For the one who knows God, there is no such thing as hopelessness. Jesus' death and resurrection gives us hope for the future, but also hope for this life. In this world. Today.

Second, Jesus longs for the day when we will all be together with Him in His Father's house. He has always been thinking of those who would believe. His heart yearns for His earthly family. His death and resurrection launched those first disciples into a gospel mission, to gather from the ends of the earth the family of believers that will enjoy God forever. And as Jesus prayed over and commissioned His disciples on His last night with them, He was praying over and commissioning us to go and tell the story to those who will believe.

John 17:24 – *Father, I desire that they also, whom You have given Me, be with Me where I am, so that they may see My glory which You have given Me, for You loved Me before the foundation of the world.*

PRAY TODAY
Dear Jesus, I am humbled by the fact that in Your darkest time, You were thinking of me. You saw beyond the cross, and were willing to experience the pain and suffering so that I could live with You forever. I never want to take that for granted. Help me to be a willing servant, commissioned by You to tell Your story. Amen.

Day Thirty-Eight: What will you do with Jesus?

Take It In

One of the criminals who were hanged there was hurling abuse at Him, saying, "Are You not the Christ? Save Yourself and us!" But the other answered, and rebuking him said, "Do you not even fear God, since you are under the same sentence of condemnation? And we indeed are suffering justly, for we are receiving what we deserve for our deeds; but this man has done nothing wrong." And he was saying, "Jesus, remember me when You come in Your kingdom!" And He said to him, "Truly I say to you, today you shall be with Me in Paradise." Luke 23:39-43

Think It Through

See our Lord Jesus – nailed to a cross. He has been lifted up, just as He said must happen: *As Moses lifted up the serpent in the wilderness, even so must the Son of Man be lifted up.* (John 3:14). His cross is not the only one on the hill, however. On either side, two thieves are crucified. One mocks. One repents.

In the repentant thief's response, we see salvation: he feared God, he recognized that he himself was under condemnation, he confessed and acknowledged his own personal sin, he recognized Jesus as the sinless sacrifice, and he asked Jesus to be merciful to him, acknowledging Him as God. For the repentant thief, it was a **good Friday**, a door opening into Paradise.

For the man who mocked Jesus, he left this earth to spend eternity separated from God. Scripture tells us that he waits in Hades for the final judgment day, after which he will be cast into the lake of fire. For the one who rejected Jesus, it was not a **good Friday**. It was the day the door closed on any possibility of good.

This brief encounter during Jesus' crucifixion perfectly illustrates what happens every time we tell the story. As Jesus is lifted up, through our words and our actions, the world is called upon to respond. They will either reject Him, mocking and dismissing us, or they will respond in repentance and faith. Our proclamation of the gospel does not save or condemn; man is already condemned, and only God saves. Our responsibility is only to lift up Jesus, and encourage others to draw near to God.

Live It Out

We find comfort in the last-minute conversion story of the thief on the cross. It gives us assurance that there is hope for our loved ones to repent, as long as they have breath. It validates the power of the cross, salvation by grace alone, through faith, and that good works are merely evidence of salvation, not the cause. But the picture we need to remember is that of Jesus lifted up between two types of people: those who will respond in repentance, and those who will reject.

The story of Jesus always demands a response. How have you responded? And how will you lift Him up today?

2 Corinthians 2:15-16 – *For we are a fragrance of Christ to God among those who are being saved and among those who are perishing; to the one an aroma from death to death, to the other an aroma from life to life. And who is adequate for these things?*

PRAY TODAY
Dear Jesus, Thank You for the mercy You showed to the thief on the cross. You give us all hope, that we can rest in Your grace and mercy, knowing that our salvation was purchased at the cross and we have done nothing to merit it or earn it. Today, we remember what You did for us on the cross. You paid my sin debt, and then drew me to Yourself. Because of that, I want to worship You with every part of my life. Show me how I can best lift You up so that the world will see You clearly. Amen.

Day Thirty-Nine: Waiting for Jesus.

Take It In

Therefore because of the Jewish day of preparation, since the tomb was nearby, they laid Jesus there. ... Now on the first day of the week Mary Magdalene came early to the tomb, while it was still dark, and saw the stone already taken away from the tomb. John 19:42; 20:1

Therefore it says, "When He ascended on high, He led captive a host of captives, and He gave gifts to men." Ephesians 4:8

Think It Through

Jesus was crucified on Friday, the day of preparation before the Sabbath. His body was laid in the tomb, and the disciples and women went back to their homes, not believing what had just happened. It certainly looked like the end. Walking away from the grave, their hearts were broken, and things looked hopeless.

God's timing was perfect. Jesus' death fulfilled all the Old Testament prophecies, even to being crucified at Passover as the lamb without blemish. And the day that His followers would spend processing His death *just happened* to be the Sabbath! By Jewish law, they would spend those hours quietly worshipping God, resting and waiting. Remember the purpose of the Sabbath? It was given by God as a gift to His people, a day to rest and remember who He is and what He has done. To honor the

74

Sabbath is a matter of trust – trust that God will accomplish all that needs to be done while we *wait* and *rest.*

What was Jesus doing during His time in the grave? According to Ephesians 4:7-10, Luke 16:19-31 and other scriptures, He descended to the place called Abraham's Bosom where Old Testament saints were waiting for the door to heaven to be opened to them. Jesus' death had paid their sin debt, and they could now enter God's presence. They had *waited* for Jesus, and were now able to enter the true Sabbath *rest.*

To the disciples, the outlook was hopeless. But what they couldn't see (yet) was that Jesus' death was only the beginning! His sacrifice had given them everything they would ever need, both for this life and for eternity. Jesus had already done the work. They just needed to *rest* in it. They just needed to *wait* to see the results!

We *rest* in the work of Christ, as we *wait* to see the results of what He has already done.

Live It Out

Do you ever feel hopeless? Are you tempted to take things in your own hands, to make things happen? Maybe God is saying *wait.* Maybe He is offering you *rest.* Trust that God, through Christ, has already accomplished what needs to be done in your life, and it may just not be time to reveal it.

Perhaps there is someone you've spoken to about Christ, but there seems to be no response. You are tempted to give up on them. Don't forget that while we are enjoying the Sabbath, the Spirit of Jesus is still working to release those held captive! We can *rest* in the finished work of Christ, and *wait* for the Spirit to act. His timing is perfect, and you never know what might happen tomorrow!

Psalm 37:7a – *Rest in the Lord and wait patiently for Him.*

PRAY TODAY
Dear Jesus, Sometimes I just don't see what You are doing. My viewpoint is limited, and I often forget that when it seems hopeless, that is when You are doing Your greatest work! Help me to trust You. Remind me to rest in You, and wait for You to act. Thank You for the work You did on the cross, and that in You, every promise of God is fulfilled. Amen.

Day Forty: The hope that comes from believing in Jesus.

Take It In

And not only this, but also we ourselves, having the first fruits of the Spirit, even we ourselves groan within ourselves, waiting eagerly for our adoption as sons, the redemption of our body. For in hope we have been saved, but hope that is seen is not hope; for who hopes for what he already sees? But if we hope for what we do not see, with perseverance we wait eagerly for it.
Romans 8:23-25

Think It Through

What if the story had ended on Saturday?

In Matthew 28, we read about two women who approached Jesus' tomb early on Sunday morning, the day we celebrate as Resurrection Day. What do you think they were thinking? Matthew tells us they **came to look at the grave.** Mark and Luke tell us they were bringing spices to anoint His body.

They expected to find a dead man.

Jesus had told them clearly when He was with them, that He must die, and would raise His body up within three days. But it was too **unbelievable**. They had watched his broken body be taken from the cross. They had been there when the tomb was sealed. They had walked away on Friday, fully convinced that **all hope was gone.** And in that same spirit of hopelessness, they approached the tomb, expecting to find things exactly the same.

How did they leave the tomb? *With great joy, running to report to the disciples.*

What changed?

They received the good news and believed it: *Jesus is alive!*

Was all hope lost, when Jesus died on the cross?
No. In surrendering to death, Jesus was paying the sin debt of the world.

Was all hope lost, when Jesus was buried?
No. In entering the grave, Jesus was victoriously releasing the Old Testament saints.

So when was hope lost? **When they didn't believe.**

Until the women *received* the news that Jesus was alive, *and **believed** it,* they were hopeless. The facts of what happened did not change. Jesus did die. Jesus was buried. Jesus did raise from the dead. What changed was their perspective of the events, and this change happened *only when they believed.*

Live It Out

Resurrection Sunday is all about the **good news that can change our life and give us hope.** Jesus is alive! He conquered sin and death, and accomplished the mission for which He was sent – to bring salvation to the world.

But before we can have hope, we must **receive** the good news, and **believe** it.

We live in a world that is dying for hope. Many people around us – our neighbors, our co-workers, our friends and family – are hopelessly lost and separated from God. The good news must be shared before it can be received and believed.

Do you know Jesus?
Have you surrendered your life to Him, confessing and repenting of your personal sin?
Are you walking daily in communion with Him?

Then you possess the hope that the world is looking for. You have the answer to every challenge, every problem, every disappointment, every failure, every addiction, every hopeless thing we face on this side of heaven.

As we think about Jesus' resurrection - the **good news** that Jesus is alive, let's commit ourselves to sharing it with the people in our lives: in your neighborhood, your office, your gym. Wherever you are, God has put you there to be a light to His salvation.

Believe it, and walk in hope. And take that **good news** out into the world and tell others that Jesus is alive, so that they too, will believe, and have hope.

Romans 15:13 - *Now may the God of hope fill you with all joy and peace in believing, so that you will abound in hope by the power of the Holy Spirit.*

PRAY TODAY
Dear Jesus, As we end this 40-day journey, I thank you for the things you have taught me about who you are. You are sovereign. You hold this world in the palm of Your hand, yet You are intimately involved in the mundane, daily details of my life! What a wonderful truth! You have divinely orchestrated where I live and work. You have put people in my sphere of influence that need Your mercy and grace, and I believe that You want to use me to share the good news about You with them. I ask that You continue to teach me to listen to Your Spirit, and obey You. Help me to walk daily in an attitude of communion and prayer so that I can hear You when You prompt me to speak or act. I pray for boldness to share with others the wonderful news that Jesus is alive! Today is all about You. I worship You, and I give myself to You to be used however You see fit. Thank You for what You did on the cross, and for choosing me to belong to You. I love You, Jesus. Amen.

Day Forty-One: Now What?

Our prayer is that during the past 40 days you have been encouraged, challenged, and blessed. If you are a follower of Christ, be bold in the knowledge that God wants to use you to share the gospel.

We hope your journey doesn't end here, but pray that the truths from God's Word will take root in your life, and bear fruit. To take what you've learned to the next level, we created ***Going Around The Corner***, a six-session Bible study for individual and group use that builds on the principles you've discovered in this devotional. This is a great "next step" to help you grow in confidence and passion for sharing the gospel. In the meantime, here are **five practical steps** you can take as a believer to implement the message of this devotional into your life today.

1. Commit to being on mission in your own neighborhood or workplace.
2. Pray specifically for God to reveal other believers in your community who will join with you.

3. Begin prayer walking, listening to God's Spirit as He speaks to you about your neighbors.
4. Act when God's Spirit prompts you. Begin serving and caring for your neighbors in practical, tangible ways.
5. Share your story as God gives you opportunities, and invite others to respond to the gospel.

If you are not a believer, here is how you can respond to Christ's invitation of salvation.

<u>Believe that God created you for a relationship with Him (believe).</u>
Genesis 1:27 – *God created man in His own image, in the image of God He created him; male and female He created them.*
Colossians 1:16 – *All things have been created through Him and for Him.*

<u>Recognize that you are separated from God (admit).</u>
Romans 3:23 - *For all have sinned and come short of the glory of God.*

<u>Be willing to turn from your sin (repent).</u>
1 John 1:9 – *If we confess our sins, He is faithful and righteous to forgive us our sins and to cleanse us from all unrighteousness.*

<u>Believe that Jesus died on the cross and rose from the grave (accept).</u>
Romans 10:9-10 – *That if you confess with your mouth Jesus as Lord, and believe in your heart that God raised Him from the dead; you will be saved; for with the heart a person believes, resulting in righteousness, and with the mouth he confesses, resulting in salvation.*

<u>Invite Jesus in to control your life through the Holy Spirit (receive).</u>
John 1:12 – *But as many as received Him, to them He gave the right to become children of God, even to those who believe in His name.*

What To Pray
Dear Jesus, I recognize that I am separated from You because of my personal sin, and I need Your forgiveness. I believe that You died on the cross to pay the penalty for my sin. I confess my sin and ask You to forgive me. By faith, I turn from my way of life to follow You instead, and accept Your gift of salvation by grace. I ask You to come into my life and transform me. Thank You for saving me and giving me eternal life. Amen.

If you sincerely prayed this prayer and surrendered your life to God, you are now His child. Please share this decision with another believer and ask them to help you get started in how to walk in your new life in Christ. We would love to hear about your decision!

Resources Available From ATCM

Going Around The Corner Bible Study
ISBN: 9780692781999 / List Price: $12.99
This six-session study helps believers explore the mission field in their own neighborhood and workplace. Learn to engage others through prayer and biblical good works guided by the prompts of the Holy Spirit. Gain confidence to evangelize through sharing the complete gospel and your own story, and discover how to establish and equip new believers in their faith. A simple, practical and biblical strategy for disciple-making.

Going Around The Corner Bible Study, Student Edition
ISBN: 9780999131831 / List Price: $9.99
A five-week study covering the first four chapters of the original study for high school and college students with expanded commentary and practical application, focusing on reaching their campus, dorm, and playing field for Christ. Students will be guided into God's Word and develop an awareness and passion for sharing the gospel.

Going Around The Corner Bible Study, Leader Guide
ISBN: 9780999131824
List Price: $3.99
Key truths for each week, helpful discussion starters and thoughtful questions to help your group apply the principles in the study, plus suggested group activities and practical application steps. Adaptable for use with the Student Edition.

40 Days of Spiritual Awareness
ISBN: 9780999131800 / List Price: $9.99
A 40-day devotional to understand who God is and how He is working in the people right around you. Each day, discover truth that will increase your awareness of God, yourself, other believers, and unbelievers. Be reminded of what is important: an awareness of God's work in our world, as He redeems and saves. At the end of the journey, you will realize that you are an important part of accomplishing that work, and be prepared to join Him.

Living In Light of the Manger
ISBN: 9780999131817 / List Price $9.99
If the manger only has meaning during our holiday celebrations, we've missed the point of the story. Jesus was born, so that we could be *born again.* The events of His birth and the people who welcomed Him have many lessons to teach us about the glorious gospel and how Jesus came to change our life. Discover the purpose and power of the manger through 40 daily devotions. Perfect to share with friends, co-workers and neighbors.

Visit aroundthecornerministries.org for these and other resources.

About The Author

Sheila Alewine came to Christ at an early age, growing up in a Baptist church in Western North Carolina. She spent a lot of time in and around church with a mom who worked as the church secretary, so marrying a full-time minister came naturally. She met her husband, Todd, while attending Liberty University in Lynchburg, VA; they married in 1985 and have spent their lives serving God together while raising two daughters.

As a young mom, Sheila fell in love with Bible study when asked to join a Precept study. Throughout the years of raising their daughters, working full-time and serving in ministry, she has loved studying and teaching in the Word. Now at this time of "empty-nest" life, she is enjoying the opportunity to try her hand at writing to encourage other believers.

Sheila and her husband reside in Hendersonville, NC, where they have established *Around The Corner Ministries* to equip and encourage followers of Christ to share the gospel where they live, work and play. They love spending time with their daughters, sons-in-law, and grandchildren.

***

Want to learn more about sharing the gospel with your neighbors? Our six-session Bible study, **Going Around The Corner**, is perfect for individual or small group study. Visit our website to order your copy!

If this devotional has made an impact on your life, please let us know by contacting us through our website **aroundthecornerministries.org**.

Around The Corner Ministries exists to take the gospel to every neighborhood in America. Our mission is to equip followers of Jesus to engage their neighborhoods and communities with the gospel of Jesus Christ.

Around The Corner Ministries is a partner to the local church, designed to teach and train Christ-followers how to evangelize their neighborhoods, workplaces, and communities. The goal is to grow healthy local churches filled with mature believers who are comfortable and passionate about sharing their faith. If you would like more information on how our ministry can partner with your local church, please contact us.